AF600041

THE CATHOLIC UNIVERSITY OF AMERICA
CANON LAW STUDIES
Number 82

ERROR INVALIDATING MATRIMONIAL CONSENT

AN HISTORICAL SYNOPSIS AND COMMENTARY

A DISSERTATION

Submitted to the Faculty of Canon Law of the Catholic University of America in Partial Fulfillment of the Requirements for the Degree of

DOCTOR OF CANON LAW

BY

HERBERT THEODORE RIMLINGER, A.B., J.C.L.,
Priest of the Diocese of Wilmington

THE CATHOLIC UNIVERSITY OF AMERICA
WASHINGTON, D. C.
1932

Nihil Obstat:

VALENTINUS T. SCHAAF, O.F.M., J.C.D.,
Censor Deputatus.
Washingtonii, D. C., die xv Maii, 1932.

Imprimatur:

EDMUNDUS J. FITZMAURICE,
Episcopus Wilmingtoniensis.
Wilmingtonii, die xviii Maii, 1932.

Printed by
THE PAULIST PRESS
New York, N. Y.

TO

HIS EXCELLENCY

THE MOST REVEREND EDMUND J. FITZMAURICE, D.D.,

Bishop of Wilmington.

TABLE OF CONTENTS

FOREWORD

THE writer of the following dissertation lays no claim to originality. All he has attempted to do, has been to interpret in English the common doctrine of canonists and theologians in regard to principles of error that invalidate matrimonial consent. At the same time, he has endeavored to point out those instances where authors are at variance in regard to certain controverted questions.

In regard to the historical synopsis of this dissertation, it will be noticed that more attention has been given to the historical development of error of servitude than to error of person and quality and simple error. The reason is evident. The history of error of person and quality begins with the time of Gratian and that of simple error traces its origin to Benedict XIV, from whose time very little legislation has been added to error of person and quality and simple error. Error of servitude, on the contrary, goes back to the early days of the Church and its historical development is necessarily much longer. However, in regard to error of servitude, since it is of little practical importance today, its historical development has been curtailed as much as possible.

Before the publication of the Code of Canon Law, error formed one of the impediments to marriage; now it has been placed among those defects that vitiate matrimonial consent. The legislation, however remains essentially the same today as before the Code. Gratian in the presentation of his theory of error relative to matrimonial consent, formulated nearly all the principles which canonists and theologians have accepted and developed within the course of time. The authors since the Code, have but reiterated the teachings of the older masters.

The writer takes this occasion to express his gratitude to his Excellency, the Most Reverend Edmund J. FitzMaurice,

D.D., Bishop of Wilmington, for the opportunity he has given him to pursue postgraduate studies in Canon Law at the Catholic University. He wishes to acknowledge his indebtedness to the learned Professors of the School of Canon Law for their practical and helpful suggestions in the writing of this dissertation, and to the Librarians of the University Library for their kindness and courtesy. He wishes to thank also the Rt. Rev. Msgr. John J. Dougherty, V.G., and the Rev. William Temple, D.D., of the Diocese of Wilmington, and Rev. Leo J. Fealy, of the Archdiocese of Baltimore, whose kindness and encouragement during the preparation of the dissertation have been greatly appreciated.

CHAPTER I

LEGISLATION BEFORE THE CODE

ARTICLE I—ERROR OF SERVITUDE FROM THE BEGINNING OF THE CHURCH UNTIL CALLISTUS I

THE present legislation of the Church in reference to error of servile condition may be traced back to the earliest days of the Church. Although this legislation has today very little practical importance, due to the comparatively small number of slaves existing in the world at present, yet, as Fourneret has pointed out, this legislation of the Church, in reference to slave marriages, is part of the legislation of the universal Church and hence, should not be without some interest.[1]

In the early days of Christianity, the Church was very much concerned with the marriages of slaves. The attitude of the Church towards slaves and their marital unions was entirely different from that of Roman Law, which denied all rights to the slave, even the right of entering into lawful marriage.[2] The Church, however, even at the outset of her divine mission, maintained that in the sight of God, all Christians were equal and that no distinction should exist between a free man and a slave.[3] Hence, the Church did not hesitate to apply this principle of equality even to a marital union that one slave contracted with another. In the strict rigor of Roman Law, such a union of two slaves could never be considered a true marriage, and it was entirely within the right of the master of

[1] Fourneret, *Le Mariage Chrétien*, p. 123.

[2] Esmein, *Le Mariage en Droit Canonique*, I, p. 350.

[3] "Ecclesia catholica cum in imperio Romano magis magisque propagaretur multosque servos Christos lucrifaceret, sevitutem nequaquam damnavit ut rem *in se* malam, sed imprimis ad iustos limites reduxit atque paulatim abrogare studuit."—Wernz-Vidal, *Jus Canon.*, V, n. 476.

the slave to break such a union at will. However, the Church, with that fearlessness which is so characteristic of her, whenever there is a principle at stake, dared to defy the Laws of Rome in proclaiming such a union lawful and valid. A little later, at the time of Callistus I, the Church went yet a step further in applying the principle of equality to slave marriages —she even sanctioned the union of a slave with a free person.[4]

Hence, in order to trace the present legislation of error in regard to servile condition of one of the parties of a marriage, it will be necessary to consider how the Church first recognized and sanctioned the marital union of two slaves, in open defiance of Roman Law, secondly, how in the course of time the Church proclaimed valid and indissoluble the union of a slave and a free man; and finally, how the Church gradually, through the course of the centuries assumed her present position in regard to the marriage of a free party and a slave.

In the New Testament itself there is nothing stated about the marriage of two slaves,[5] and to ascertain the mind of the Church in regard to this question, there must be consulted the early legislation of the Church, which is found in the so-called Apostolic Canons. It is, indeed, true that many of these canons which are now in existence, such as the Apostolic Constitutions are, of a spurious character, but they exhibit at least the mind of the Church during the early centuries of her existence.[6] The eighth canon of the Apostolic Constitutions not only recognizes slave marriages, but lays it down as an offense, if a master of a slave who has been guilty of fornication, does not give him a slave for a wife. If a slave man or a woman have a wife or husband, let them learn to be content

[4] Allard, *Les Esclaves Chrétien*, p. 290.

[5] Fulton, *The Laws of Marriage*, p. 102; Knecht, *Handbuch des Katholischen Eherechts*, p. 559; Wernz-Vidal, *Jus Canon.*, V, n. 476; Linneborn, *Grundriss des Eherechts*, p. 272.

[6] Ayrinhac, *General Legislation in the New Code of Canon Law*, p. 28; Allard, *Les Esclaves Chrétien*, p. 283; Van Hove, *Prolegomena*, n. 106.

with one another; but if they be unmarried, let them learn not to commit fornication, but to enter into lawful marriage. If one of the faithful knows that his slave is guilty of fornication and does not give him a wife, let him be accursed.[7]

It is clearly evident then how the Church early recognized the marriage of slaves and this indeed, was a great and daring thing to do. For according to Roman Law, the slave was considered as chattle, had not rights whatsoever, could enter into no bond of marriage and depended absolutely upon the will of his master.[8] He was allowed, however, a kind of contubernium, but this union had no lasting effect and could be broken any time at the will of the master.[9] But the Church, on the contrary, following the teaching of her Divine Founder who had raised marriage to the dignity of a sacrament, gave the slave free access to all her sacraments, and by a simple gesture asserted that all without distinction could partake of the sacrament of matrimony. Hence, the Church at this point broke with Roman Law, and proclaimed that the marriage of two slaves was on an equal with that of the haughty aristocrat whose marriage was protected so severely by Roman Law.[10] Thus within the first few centuries of the Church's existence, the independence of Christian marriage was maintained and the Church proclaimed, as she has done so ever since, that while the state is supreme in its own sphere of activity, it has no right over Christian marriages.[11] While Roman Law denied marriage to the slave, the Church, sanctioned his marriage and

[7] Mansi. I, 579.

[8] *A Dictionary of Christian Antiquity,* I, 449; Bonfante, *Institutioni di Diritto Romano,* p. 38; Buckland, *A Text-Book of Roman Law,* p. 63; Girard, *Droit Romain,* p. 99; Sherman, *Roman Law in the Modern World,* II, 202.

[9] *A Dictionary of Christian Antiquity,* I, 450; Bonfante, *Istituzioni di Diritto Romano,* p. 38.

[10] Allard, *Les Esclaves Chrétien,* p. 284; Fulton, *The Laws of Marriage,* p. 104; Freisen, *Geschichte des Canonishchen Eherechts,* p. 282.

[11] C. 1016.

considered it to be at once a stable and perpetual union, distinct and entirely free from the power of the Roman Law.

It can easily be imagined, what effect and influence such a new and benign doctrine had upon the slaves during the early centuries of the Church's existence. The Roman Law did not recognize the slave's right to marriage, because according to Roman Law, the slave was devoided of all rights whatsoever. But the Church recognized the slave's right to enter into lawful marriage; to defy his master when that master wished him to dissolve his marital union and enter into another.[12]

It was no wonder, then, that so many slaves from the First Century, turned in conversion towards the Church that held out such advantages to them. For the Church restored to the slave two rights, the right of his conscience and the right of his person and made him in all fundamental things of human life equal to the free. The Church recognized his marital union as indissoluble. Hardly can it be wondered at, that those slaves who were not entirely corrupt should have found such an appeal from the early Church.[13]

While the Church early recognized the marriage of two slaves and while she held such a union as sacred and indissoluble as the union of a man and woman who were free, what was her position in regard to the marital union of a free man and his slave? Here the Church did not come in conflict with Roman Law.[14] For, although Roman Law did not recognize such a union as lawful marriage, yet it was tolerated by Roman Law and held to be entirely honorable. Hence, the Church, in recognizing such a union as a true marriage only recognized what Roman Law already tolerated and furthermore, a rescript of Antonius said that a man entering into a union with the

[12] Esmein, *Le Mariage en Droit Canonique,* 351; Allard, *Les Esclaves Chrétien,* p. 284; Wallon, *Histoire de l'Esclavage dans l'Antiquite,* p. 105.

[13] Allard, "Slavery," *The Catholic Encyclopedia,* XIV, 37.

[14] Freisen, *Geschichte des Canonishchen Eherechts,* p. 282; Bonfante, *Instituzioni di Diritto Romano,* p. 40; Girard, *Droit Romain,* p. 100.

slave of another was liable to no punishment.[15] The Church even recognized the union of a female slave with her master. For although the Church during the first centuries was strongly opposed to the marriage of a pagan and a Christian and considered such a union as one of the worst evils, yet once a slave who was thus joined to her pagan master was converted to the Church, the Church recognized her union as indissoluble. This is stated clearly in the eighth canon of the Apostolic Constitutions.[16]

"The concubine slave of a pagan master ought, if she be united to him alone, to be received into the Church. But if at the same time she has abandoned herself to others, let her be rejected."

The Church in this respect, followed the Roman Law in considering the intention of the parties who thus entered into such unions, since in Roman Law the intention of the parties made a marital union of this kind either a lawful concubinage or a simple liaison.[17] If the Church were convinced, that there had been an intention of entering into a lawful concubinage, then the Church sanctioned such a union. But the Church in regard to this particular question, again took a stand against Roman Law, for once having recognized such a lawful concubinage the Church held it to be an indissoluble union. Roman Law, on the contrary, permitted the master of the slave to break such a union at will. The slave in the eyes of the Church, however, was considered as joined to an indissoluble marriage and should her master leave her or repudiate her, she was never to marry again while her master was still living.[18]

If Roman Law tolerated the union of a free man and a

[15] *Code Just.*, VII, XV, 13.

[16] Mansi, I, 579.

[17] Girard, *Droit Roman.*, p. 162; Buckland, *A Text-Book of Roman Law*, p. 112; Bonfante, *Istituzioni di Diritto Romano*, p. 173.

[18] Allard, *Les Esclaves Chrétien*, p, 288; Fulton, *Laws of Marriage*, p. 106; Wallon, *Histoire de l'Esclavage dans l'Antiquite*, p. 108.

slave, on the contrary, it was strongly opposed to the union of a slave and a free woman.[19] Constantine declared that any commerce of a matron with a slave, should be punished and no legal bond could result from it, not even a lawful concubinage.

The union of a free woman and the slave of another was more severely frowned upon. According to a decree of Claudius, the matron who was guilty of this commerce was forced to lose her liberty or at least her title of honor.[20]

It must be confessed however, that this decree of Claudius was little observed and at the time of the Emperor Vespasian, it had already fallen into desuetude. This emperor however, recalled it into practice and Constantine renewed it, only later to abrogate it himself.[21]

But the law, however, still remained on the statutes that the commerce of a free woman with her slave could be bound by no matrimonial bond and the commerce of a free woman with the slave of another constituted in the eyes of the law a heinous crime.

It is evident then that the union of a free woman with a man of servile condition was strongly opposed by Roman Law. But there existed a very peculiar and delicate situation in Rome at the beginning of the third century which determined the early Church to legislate contrary to Roman Law on this particular subject. It was at this period of the Church's existence that many converts came flowing into the early Church but the proportion of women over men was great.[22] The reason for this is easily explained. Although many men at this particular epoch were fully convinced that the Christian religion was alone true, nevertheless, they could not bring themselves to em-

[19] *Theod. Cod.*, lib. 3, tit. 7 *de Nupiis* Leg. I; Bingham, *Antiquities of the Christian Church*, II, 1206.

[20] *Cod. Justin*, lib. v, tit. IV, 23.

[21] Allard, *Les Esclaves Chrétien*, p. 289; Bingham, *Antiquities of the Christian Church*, II, p. 1208.

[22] Allard, *Les Esclaves Chrétien*, p. 289.

brace a religion which by its tenents debarred them from practically all public functions and honors since the public life of the Romans was so intimately associated with every kind of idolatrous worship.

Since then many of these converts were young noble women, where were they to seek their future husbands? During the first centuries of her existence, the Christian Church was deadly opposed to the marriage of a pagan and a Christian because she knew from bitter experience, how terrible were the evils inflicted by pagan husbands upon their wives converted to the Christian religion.[23]

Many of the young women converts of this period found themselves faced with a very trying situation. For while they wished to obey the stringent demands of the Church in thus avoiding a marriage with a pagan yet they were unwilling to sacrifice their social position by marrying husbands lower in rank, since Roman Law forbade noble women to enter into a marriage with one who was not an aristocrat. Under Marcus Aurelius and Commodus, a decree was passed, that if a widow or a daughter of a senator should marry one who was not of the best blood, she should lose her title and be prohibited from passing this title on to her children.[24]

A way, however, seemed open to these young noble women who wished to obey the Church and at the same time keep their title and rank in pagan society.[25] These women began to imitate the practice of the pagan women of their day. For although at this epoch of Roman history, the marriage bond was

[23] "Le concile d'Illiberis appelle le mariage de'une Chrétienne et d'un païen 'un adultère de l'ame. L'experience des persécutions avait appris aux premiers fidèles à se défier de telles unions. On avait vu des maris épier les secrets de leur femmes Chrétiennes et les livrer aux persécuteur: d'autres trainer eux-memes leur femme a l'autel des faux dieux, lui tenir la main pour la contraindre a offrir l'éncens, malgré les protestations de la malheureuse."—Allard, *Les Esclaves Chrétien*, p. 292.

[24] *Gai. Insti.* I, 65; Fulton, *The Laws of Marriage*, p. 107.

[25] Allard, *Les Esclaves Chretien*, p. 292.

very light and divorce could easily be procured, yet many of the young Roman women were unwilling to submit themselves to husbands of equal rank. Hence, they sought husbands from either among the slaves or the freedmen who, in no way, could oppose their wills, since these men were either their own slaves or owed all their fortune to them. Hence, there is to be found here a strange anomaly in the Roman Law of this period.[26] For although Roman Law considered a union of a free woman with either a slave or a freedman illegal, and although it did not even deem such a union as lawful concubinage, yet it did not, at this period of history attribute to such a union any crime. Another fortunate circumstance for these young noble women was the fact that such a union could be broken at will without the least detriment to themselves. It would have been different, however, had these noble women joined themselves to free men who were not of an aristocratic state of life. In such a case, they would have lost their title.

With the example of their pagan sisters before them, and wishing at the same time to preserve their rank and obey the strict mandates of the Church, many of these young women converts from paganism began to marry their slaves or freedmen of the Christian religion. In this way, they still retained their title and honor and at the same time avoided a union with one who was not a Christian. But a doubt began to be engendered in the minds of these young converts. Although the Roman Law did not punish such a union, yet it in no way recognized it as lawful concubinage. Would the Church, then, recognize this union as lawful marriage? It was here that the Church again dared to assume a position contrary to Roman Law. For just as the Church had proclaimed the marriage of two slaves, a marriage as sacred as that of the haughty aristocrat and his wife, so now in contradiction to Roman Law, the Church proclaimed a union of a noble woman with a slave or a

[26] Döllinger, *Hippolytus and Callistus*, p. 147.

freedman, just as truly a marriage as that which existed between two noble Romans or between two free people of whatever rank.[27]

The Pope who dared in the name of the Church to proclaim the validity of such marriages was Callistus I who as tradition relates, was a slave himself before raised to the dignity of the priesthood. His action in proclaiming such marriages as valid and lawful provoked much bitter criticism from some of the Bishops of the Church. Hippolytus maintained that Callistus I, in declaring such marriages valid, was a cooperator in the many evils which resulted from them. For many pagan women who had contracted such marriages blushed at their offspring and in order to obliterate from themselves a certain odium with which society branded them, were lead to procure abortion. It is stated that some of the Christian women, after marrying a freedman or slave fell into the same abuses, but this certainly cannot be laid to the blame of Callistus I. He but enunciated a clear principle that such unions, if entered into, with the right intentions were lawful and sacred and it is very probable if he had not sanctioned them, they would have lead to worse evils and more startling abuses.[28]

Article II—Error of Servitude From Callistus I to the Code

It has been seen, that the Church recognized the marriage of slaves and also held that the marriage of two slaves, valid and properly entered into, was as sacred as the marriage of two free people. There has also been noticed a peculiar phenomenon under Callistus I, how that Supreme Pontiff of the Church came to the aid of the young maidens converted to the Church from paganism, and recognized their unions as

[27] Döllinger, *Hippolytus and Callistus,* p. 160.

[28] Allard, *Les Esclaves Chrétien,* p. 295; Fulton, *Laws of Marriage,* p. 107; Wallon, *Histoire de l'Esclavage dans l'Antiquite,* p. 109.

valid with their slaves, provided they really intended to enter into a true matrimonial union. But while the Church recognized as valid the marriage of slaves, for many centuries yet, she continued to demand the consent of the master of the slave.[29] This principle is verified in one of the canons of the Fourth Council of Orleans [30] for it lays down a definite ruling that the slaves who flee to the sanctuary of the Church in an attempt to pledge their troth without the consent of their masters, shall be forced to return and that their unions shall be dissolved, provided they have not, in the meantime, obtained the consent of their masters. However, the Council further prescribes, if consent of the master or masters, as the case may be, have been granted, the marriage must not later be attempted to be dissolved by the master. Hence, the Church guarded the marriage bond of the slaves who had validly entered into the holy state of marriage.[31] But after the middle of the eighth century, from the Council of Verberie (752) the marriage of two slaves came to be considered valid even without the consent of the master of the slaves.[32] This was but a logical sequence of the principle that the consent of the parents was no longer required for the valid marriage of children.

While the Church came to recognize the marriage of two slaves as valid without the consent of the master what was her attitude to the union of a free person and a slave after the time of Callistus I? It has been seen how this Pontiff allowed and sanctified the union of a noble woman with a slave, but from the subsequent legislation of the Church, this seems to have been but a passing legislation; for a century later, after the persecution had died away, this peculiar situation which

[29] Esmein, *Le Mariage en Droit Canonique,* I, 350; Cappello, *De Sacram.,* III, n. 591.

[30] Mansi, IX, 117.

[31] Esmein, *Le Mariage en Droit Canonique,* I, 352.

[32] Allard, "Slavery." *The Catholic Encyclopedia,* XIV, 38; Lombard, *Sent.,* lib. IV, D. XXXII.

faced the young women converted to the Church at the time of Callistus I, did not then exist. Leo I, in his celebrated letter to Rusticus,[33] shows what policy the Church pursued in regard to these unions. He says in this letter, if a man leave his slave concubine and take a woman who is free, he is at liberty to do so and a cleric who gives his daughter to such a man does not commit any reprehensible act. Pope Leo I bases his arguments upon the Scriptures and also upon the principles of Roman Law.

It was still the law that prompted Gregory I [34] to write to a certain cleric and command him to put away his wife when that Pontiff had heard that she was of servile condition. However, when a wife of the same cleric proved that she was not a slave, she was promptly ordered to be restored to the cleric by order of the same Pontiff.

It must be noted too in the twelfth century that the Visigoth Law, which well reflects the spirit of those times, strongly reproved the marriage of a person of free birth with one of servile condition. Moreover, the punishment that was given to parties who had violated this law could not be compared in cruelty to that of the Roman Law.[35]

But a strong reaction against the rigorous laws bearing on the marriage of a free person with a slave, gradually set in. Several factors contributed to bring about this reaction. The status of the slave had now become nothing worse than that of a free man of low social position. The true principles of Christianity, maintaining that all men were free before the throne of God, had within the course of time, sunk deep into the consciousness of the people. Again much importance was attached to a canon which Gratian, in his collection, attributes

[33] C. 12, C. XXXII, q. 2; Esmein, *Le Mariage en Droit Canonique,* I, 356.

[34] C. 5, C. XXIX, q. 2.

[35] Esmein, *Le Mariage en Droit Canonique,* I, 358; *Dictionary of Ancient Antiquity,* p. 1093; Poullet, *Histoire Politique en Belgeque,* I, 655.

to Julius II.[36] This canon held that a free person was able to marry with one of servile condition. But the canon presupposes that the free person knew before the marriage that the other party was a slave.[37] This is, also, the sense of the Canons of the Councils of Verberie [38] and Compiègne.[39]

But what if error had been made in regard to the servile condition of the slave? This was a very difficult and delicate situation that thus confronted canonists and theologians. A solution of this problem will be found in the CCXI Letter of Yves.[40] In this letter, Yves maintains that a marriage of a free person with a slave, is valid and indissoluable, even when the free party enters into the union in ignorance of the servile condition of the other party. Yves maintained that the ancient legislation of the Popes and the Civil Law, both among the Romans and among subsequent nations, was wrong, because from natural law, nothing prohibits a free party from marrying a slave. But this theory of Yves involved difficulties and inconveniences, for according to the customs of the people, a free woman who would attempt a union with a slave, was reduced to slavery herself.[41] Moreover, if such a marriage were valid, then the free party was obliged to enter into common life with the one of servile condition and, as such a one, was not able to leave his place of servitude, the free party must perforce, go to the abode of the slave. In attempting to avoid this logical consequence, Yves maintained in the same letter, that the free party who had thus erred was not obliged to cohabit with the slave or render the common life, but the bond still remained intact.

[36] C. 1, C. XXIX, q. 2.

[37] Allard, "Slavery," *The Catholic Encyclopedia*, XIV, 38; Esmein, *Le Mariage en Droit Canonique*, I, 358.

[38] Mansi, XII, 526.

[39] Mansi, XII, 657.

[40] Quoted by Esmein, *Le Mariage en Droit Canonique*, I, 361.

[41] Poullet, *Histoire Politique en Belgeque*, I, 660; *Dictionary of Ancient Antiquity*, p. 1095.

This, however, was hardly a satisfactory solution and Yves had no difficulty in seeing it. He then proposed, in the CCXLII Letter that such a marriage of a free party with a slave, was null when the free party before the marriage was not cognizant of the servile condition of the other party.[42] He based his solution on the fact that a marriage in which a free party is lead into slavery, does not represent the love of Christ for His Church and hence, such a marriage could not be a sacrament.

Yves, however, was violently taken to task for his second opinion by Audoin, the Bishop of Evreux, who reproved him for annulling the marriage of a free person and a slave.[43] Yves was now forced to defend himself and quoted the celebrated letter of Leo I. to Rusticus and also the Twenty-second Novel of Justinian, where it is stated that if a free man marry a slave, erring in regard to her servile condition, no marriage could exist. But the two authors, quoted by Yves, would rather suppose that a marriage with a slave were invalid at all times. Yves did not care to go so far, for he maintained if the free party knew of the servile condition, the marriage was valid. To support this view, Yves relied upon this feeble sort of reasoning; namely, if the free party knows the other to be a slave, then, his consent is free and such a marriage is joined by God and not by man. On the contrary, if the free party is not aware that he is marrying a slave, then his consent is not free and man, rather than God, joins the two and God separates them. It might be stated here that the great stress Yves places upon the Twenty-second Novel, does not help to establish the validity of a marriage, when the free party knows of the servile condition of the other spouse. This novel merely states the fact that in case of error there is no marriage. It does not

[42] Esmein, *Le Mariage en Droit Canonique,* I, 362.
[43] Esmein, *Le Mariage en Droit Canonique,* I, 362.

consider the case where the freeman marries a slave whose servile condition is known to him before the marriage.[44]

It was this last opinion of Yves that came to triumph in the course of time. But it was to take, however, more solid juridical shape. Peter Lombard [45] attempted to do it. In the case of a slave marrying a free person, the slaves were to be considered as an intermediary class between those able to marry and those absolutely incapable of marriage. If a free party did not know of this condition, then the party of servile condition was incapable of marriage.

Peter Lombard deemed that the annulment of such a marriage was a punishment rendered to the slave who was in most cases prompted fraudulently to represent himself as free in order to marry the free party. This reasoning of Peter Lombard [46] was very ingenious but at the same time, very subtle, for the validity of the marriage rested upon the ignorance or knowledge of the free party as to the free state of the intended spouse. But still this was not quite satisfactory and Peter Lombard eventually came to base it upon error and so in his theory of error, he places error of servile condition. But, like Gratian, he considered it of such importance as to devote a special treatment to it.[47]

The Interpreters of the Decree of Gratian, taking up the question of error of servile condition, eventually came to the conclusion that every slave was fully capable of marrying a free person [48] but where the free party had erred relative to the condition of the slave, the marriage was null. Alexander III, Urban III, and Innocent III,[49] adhered to this view and the impediment of servile condition resolved itself to this, that the

[44] Esmein, *Le Mariage en Droit Canonique,* I, 363.

[45] Lombard, *Sent.,* lib. IV, D. XXXIV, Cap. I.

[46] Lombard, *Sent.,* IV, D. XXXIV, Cap. I.

[47] Esmein, *Le Mariage en Droit Canonique,* I, 364.

[48] Freisen, *Geschichte des Canonischen Eherechts,* p. 290.

[49] C. 2-4, X, *De Conj. serv.,* IV, 2.

slave was freely capable of marrying a free person, but the quality of servile condition was judged a quality so important that it was placed on a par with substantial error and thus destroyed a true consent of marriage.[50]

From this time onward, until our day, the theory of error of servile condition has remained the same. For many centuries, it was held by canonists and theologians as a diriment impediment. The Code, however, ceased to recognize it as an impediment to marriage and merely placed it in that section of the Code which deals with defects of matrimonial consent.[51] However, the legislation now governing error of servile condition, remains the same as before the Code.

Article III—Error of Person and Quality

In the Old Testament, there is found only one reference to error regarding matrimonial consent and this occurs in the twenty-ninth chapter of Genesis. The marriage of Jacob and Lia is often quoted by Canonists and Theologians as an apt example of error of person. Apart from this one example there is no other reference either to error of person or quality in the Old Testament.

The theory of error of person and quality in reference to the consent of marriage was developed late among ecclesiastical writers. So far no canons can be found before the time of Gratian that have any reference to error of person and quality.[52] The theory was first proposed in the Twelfth Century.[53] It is to be found in the works of two of the greatest ecclesiastical writers of their age, Gratian[54] a Canonist, and

[50] Esmein, *Le Mariage en Droit Canonique*, I, 365.

[51] C. 1083.

[52] Wernz-Vidal, *Jus Matrimonium*, p. 556; Freisen, *Geschichte des Canonischen Eherechts*, p. 277.

[53] Esmein, *Le Mariage en Droit Canonique*, I, 344.

[54] C. XXIX, q. 1.

Peter Lombard, [55] a Theologian. In taking up their works, in reference to the theory of error, one is impressed immediately by the striking similarity of their treatment. They use the same examples, the same terms, the same principles, in fact the only difference is, that Gratian is more ample in his development and the order pursued by each writer differs in some respects. The similarity of their treatment leads one to presume that the doctrine of error laid down in these two works was developed anteriorily to them, but as yet there has been no evidence of this.[56] Gratian and Peter Lombard both distinguish error into four kinds; error of person, error of quality, error of fortune and error of condition. This division is not based upon extraordinary or scientific principles [57] but so great is the force of the tradition behind this theory of error, that nearly every civil code that treats of error in regard to the consent of marriage has kept the first three divisions.

In propounding his theory of error, Gratian first proposes an argument in which he lays down a case of a certain noble woman. This woman has been informed that she is to be sought in marriage by a nobleman whom she has never seen. While she awaits his arrival, a slave presents himself to her as the expected bridegroom and the lady, thus deceived, enters into a marriage with him. After the marriage has been celebrated, the true bridegroom appears and now demands the woman for his wife. Having perceived that she has been deceived by the slave, the woman desires to leave him and marry the nobleman. Gratian then asks two questions, first, if there has been a marriage between the woman and the slave, secondly, if the woman may immediately abandon the slave when she realizes that she has been deceived.[58]

[55] Lombard, *Sent.*, lib. IV, D. XXXI.
[56] Esmein, *Le Mariage en Droit Canonique,* I, 345.
[57] Esmein, *Le Mariage en Droit Canonique,* I, p. 345.
[58] C. XXIX, q. 1.

In response to the first question, Gratian has a long dictum in which he exposes his theory of error regarding the consent of marriage. Though these principles of error are here for the first time put down in an accurate form, Gratian does not trouble himself to give us any authority for his statements.[59] It is in the first part of this dictum that Gratian is concerned primarily in establishing the principle that matrimonial consent can be destroyed by error. Marriage, says Gratian, is a union of a man and woman who have joined themselves together to live a common life. In order that this union may be brought about, the consent of both parties is necessary. Here one finds Gratian employing the principles of buying and selling as found in Roman Law, but he does not make mention of it.[60] Consent, Gratian says, following the Roman principles, is of two or more persons in reference to the same object. But he who has erred has not perceived, hence, he has not consented, that is, he has not perceived simultaneously with the others. In the case quoted above, concerning the woman deceived by the slave, Gratian holds that the woman did not give a true consent to the slave and therefore, there was no marriage. In order to make this point clear, Gratian takes as example, error regarding the ordination of a priest.[61] If a young man places himself before one whom he erroneously thinks is a bishop, such a man, says Gratian, must yet be ordained by a bishop, since he has not yet been ordained. In like manner, this woman has yet to be married, since she has not given her true consent. But here Gratian shows how uncertain are his notions of error.[62] In the above case of the candidate for holy orders, the

[59] Freisen, *Geschichte des Canonischen Eherechts*, p. 277.

[60] L, 1, 2, D. (2-14).

[61] C. XXIX, q. 1.

[62] "Gleich hier zeigt Gratian, wie unklar seine Begriffe von *error* sind; denn es bedarf kaum der Erwähnung, dass das beigefügte Beispiel nicht passt; nicht der *error* macht in solchem Falle die Weihe ungiltig, sonders die fehlende Eigenschaft des Ordinirenden als episcopus."—Freisen, *Geschichte des Canonischen Eherechts*, p. 277.

invalidity of his ordination is not due to any error of his, but rather to the fact that the man to whom he presented himself for ordination lacked the character of the episcopacy.[63]

Having now proved that error can destroy the matrimonial consent, Gratian proceeds to enumerate the various kinds of error that have reference to consent and shows that of these four kinds of error, only two destroy consent of marriage. The four kinds of error given by Gratian are: Error of Person, which occurs when one thinks this man is "Virgil," whereas in reality he is "Paul"; Error of Fortune, which arises in the case where one of the parties deems the other rich, when it is later found that he is poor or less wealthy than had been anticipated; Error of Quality, when a man marries a corrupt woman or a prostitute, believing her to be chaste or a virgin; finally, Error of Servile Condition, which happens when a slave is mistaken for a free person.

Only Error of Person and Error of Condition, asserts Gratian, will destroy consent. In order to help prove this statement, Gratian this time presents examples culled from civil law. If the owner of a field bargains to sell it to Marcellus and another represents himself as Marcellus and buys the field, it cannot be said that the owner really consented to sell him the field. Again, if I wish to buy gold from a man and this man, in the transaction of the sale, substitutes brass, no one will say that I desired to buy brass. For in this case I did not consent to the purchase of brass but rather to the purchase of the gold.[64]

Here Gratian pauses to meet an objection that might be raised against the marriage of Jacob and Lia.[65] It is stated in the Scriptures that Jacob desired to marry his cousin Rachel, but his crafty father-in-law, having promised Jacob the daugh-

[63] Freisen, *Geschichte des Canonischen Eherechts*, p. 277.

[64] C. XXX, q. 1; Esmein, *Le Mariage en Droit Canonique*, I, 345.

[65] Genesis, 29:16-28.

ter he desired, fraudulently offered his oldest daughter Lia. This fraud Jacob did not perceive until the following morning. Here is apparently a fine example of error of person but it must be remembered that Jacob kept Lia for his wife. In order then to reconcile this evident example of error of person and the subsequent union, Gratian, with much subtlety [66] distinguishes consent into antecedent and subsequent. The former precedes the carnal copulation and the latter follows it. In the case of Jacob and Lia, Jacob did not give antecedent but subsequent consent and so his marriage with Lia was a real marriage. Gratian also excuses both Jacob and Lia from any fornicatious concubinage because both had erred and the error destroyed the imputability of a bad action.[67]

In the last part of the long dictum, Gratian turns his attention to error of fortune and error of quality, maintaining that neither of these two kinds of error can vitiate the matrimonial consent. This time, Gratian quotes an example from ecclesiastical law. Thus if a man accepts a benefice of a church which he thinks will give him a very profitable income, and later he finds the income is very little, then, this man has erred, but he must still retain the benefice. Gratian applies this principle to error of quality in marriage. If one of the parties before the marriage believes the other to be wealthy, and it later develops that the supposed wealthy party is poor, or possesses less wealth than anticipated, there has been error, but this error does not destroy matrimonial consent. In order yet more to drive home the truth of this principle, Gratian contrasts this error of quality in marriage to error in the purchase of a field. Thus, says Gratian, if a man wishes to buy a field which he believes fertile, only to find after the sale that it is useless and barren, he has erred but he has no recourse

[66] C. XXIX, q. 1.

[67] Freisen, *Geschichte des Canonischen Eherechts*, p. 278; *Summa Theol.*, p. III, Suppl. q. 51, art 1 ad 5.

against the one who sold him the field. In like manner, the man who marries a corrupt woman, believing her to be a woman of good repute, errs, but this error does not affect his matrimonial consent.

For the above statement, Gratian gives no authority and, as far as can be seen, no authority previous to Gratian can be found.[68] Canon 10 of the Council of Compiègne 757, might apply here because it is laid down in this Council that "si quis uxorem accepit et eam contaminatam inveniens dereliquit et aliam accepit, statutum est, ut omnimodis ad priorem revertatur, quia et ipse, quando illam accepit, potest fieri, ut virgo non esset."[69] This canon would seem to lend authority to Gratian's statement but, on the contrary, Canon 10 of the same council permits a man to leave his wife who has been contaminated by his brother, and enter into a new union. There are here apparently, two conflicting statements, but this last canon is according to the authority of Freisen not authentic.[70]

Turning attention now to Gratian's great contemporary, Peter Lombard, one finds the identical theory of error set forth in the work of the master of the Sentences.[71] Peter Lombard presents his theory of error of person, fortune and quality in nine short sentences, devoting a whole separate question to error of servile condition. While Gratian in his theory of error gives more examples and follows a more logical order than Peter Lombard, the latter's theory, however, is essentially the same as Gratian's. He begins like Gratian in maintaining that not all error invalidates consent and after narrating the four

[68] Freisen, *Geschichte des Canonischen Eherechts*, p. 279.

[69] Mansi, XII, p. 657.

[70] "Nach der Einrichtung der Sammlung Regino's is der Canon wohl nicht von Regino in diesem Sinne gefälscht, sonder es ist die Annahme gerechtfertigt, dass er irgendwo die Stelle in dieser corrupten Gestalt vorfand und aufnahm."—Freisen, *Geschichte des Canonischen Eherechts*, p. 279; Hefele, *Conciliengesch*, III, 59.

[71] Peter Lombard, *Sent.*, lib. IV, D. XXX, tit. I.

kinds of error that refer to matrimonial consent, says that of these four, only error of person and error of servile condition invalidates a marriage. In the same manner as Gratian, Peter Lombard gives no authority for his statements, in fact, unlike Gratian he does not at times give any reason for his statements, but merely lays down the principles. "Non autem omnis error consensum impedit. . . . Error fortunae et qualitatis consensum non excludit. . . ." The example that Peter Lombard gives to prove that error of person destroys consent is, like Gratian, taken from Roman Law in regard to the principles of buying and selling. Thus he gives as example, a case in which a man wishes to buy gold has been sold brass. But here, Peter Lombard as well as Gratian does not consider this error as referring to the individuality of the person of the contract, but rather to the matter of the contract. The same objection of the marriage of Jacob and Lia is presented and shortly dismissed by the explanation similar to that of Gratian, that matrimonial consent may be antecedent and subsequent. Peter Lombard maintains that either consent makes the marriage valid and since Jacob gave subsequent consent, this easily explains the fact that Lia remaining in Jacob's household, was his true wife.[72]

The theory of error regarding person, quality, fortune and servile condition was now well established and entered definitely into Canon Law.[73] However, in the course of time yet another peculiar kind of error was added to the list. Both Gratian and Peter Lombard had maintained that no error of quality was able to destroy matrimonial consent. The canonists coming after these two great masters, concentrating much of their attention upon error of person, began to consider that it was really the error of the individuality of the person rather than the error of the matter of the contract, which destroyed con-

[72] Freisen, *Geschichte des Canonischen Eherechts*, p. 278.

[73] Esmein, *Le Mariage en Droit Canonique*, I, 346.

sent. Hence, arose the theory that a quality could destroy consent of marriage whenever this quality was of such a kind that it corresponded to error of the individuality of the person. St. Thomas, in his treatment of error, takes up this question,[74] and although he cannot be called the first who treats of this peculiar kind of error, yet to him is given the credit of formulating the terminology which now is associated therewith.[75] St. Thomas calls this error, error of quality redounding to error of person. It consists in this, that if error in matrimonial consent rests upon a quality which is peculiar to a certain person, so that it might be considered identical to the individuality of a certain person, then such an error destroys matrimonial consent. But, as St. Thomas points out, the consent of marriage must be directly given to that quality of the person rather than to the person here and now present.[76] For instance, if the son of a king or the first born child of a nobleman presents himself before a young woman and asks her hand in marriage, it is necessary that the young woman really wish to marry the son of the king, or the eldest child of the nobleman. If she is not concerned with his lineage and wishes only to marry the man who presents himself before her, and she later discovers that this man is neither the son of a king nor the first son of a nobleman, such error does not destroy the consent of marriage. The latter kind of error is but simple error of quality. But error redounding to error of person is primarily concerned with the individuality of the person.[77]

[74] *Summa Theol.*, p. III, Suppl. p. 51, art 1 ad 5; Esmein, *Le Mariage en Droit Canonique*, 347; Freisen, *Geschichte des Canonischen Eherechts*, p. 278.

[75] Wernz-Vidal, *Jus Matrim.*, p. 556; Gasparri, *De Matrim.*, n. 896.

[76] "Unde si consensus mulieris feratur in istam personam directe, error nobilitatis ipsius non impedit matrimonium; si autem directe intendit consentire in filium regis, quicumque sit ille, tunc si alius praesentetur ei quam filius regis, est error personae, et impedietur matrimonium."—*Summa Theol.*, p. III, Suppl. 51, art 2 ad 5.

[77] Freisen, *Geschichte des Canonischen Eherechts*, p. 278.

In the collection of the Decretals, although there is a special title given to error of servile condition, nothing is said in reference to the impediment of error of person. However, the impediment is understood.[78]

Article IV—Simple Error

The last kind of error, affecting matrimonial consent, to be considered in the historical development of error is the error of the unity, indissolubility and sacramental dignity of marriage. The accurate presentation of this theory was of a much later date, in fact it was not until the time of Benedict XIV that there is found a well presented treatment of this error. There is a somewhat vague reference to it in a letter of Innocent III, (Circa 1212).[79] This Pontiff was asked what attitude the Church should take in regard to a marriage of which one of the parties, after the marriage, lapses into heresy or infidelity. Innocent III while making a comparison of this marriage to a marriage that has been dissolved by virtue of the Pauline Privelege, replies that the marriage cannot be dissolved, because, says the Pontiff, if a dissolution of this kind were allowed, many would simulate heresy, in order to have their marriages dissolved by the Church.

Although Innocent III seems to have referred to the error, it was not until Benedict XIV that there is found an accurate presentation of the theory of error of the indissolubility, unity and the sacramental dignity of marriage.[80] The question arose in regard to those marriages of Protestants and Greeks, who, falsely interpreting the words of St. Matthew's Gospel[81] in regard to the indissolubility of marriage, maintained that a

[78] Wernz-Vidal, *Jus Matrimonium*, p. 557; C. 18, 26, X de sponsal, IV, I.
[79] C. 7, X *de divort.*, IV, 19.
[80] Benedict XIV, *De Synod. dioec.*, lib. XIII, cap. 22, n. 3.
[81] Mathew, 13:24.

marriage could be dissolved on account of the infidelity or adultery of the other party. In regard to this question, Benedict XIV held that all such marriages were valid, as long as there did not exist at the time of the marriage, a positive act of the will, excluding one of the essential properties of marriage. For although one or both of the contracting parties falsely believe that marriage is a dissoluble union, yet as long as they have a general intention of contracting marriage, according to the mind of Christ, they contract a real marriage. In this case, says Benedict XIV, a private error cannot destroy the general intention of contracting a valid marriage. Hence, the validity of the marriage thus depends upon the general intention of contracting a valid marriage.[82]

Since the time of Benedict XIV, nothing new has been added to the legislation of the Church, regarding error invalidating matrimonial consent. The general principles of error of person and quality in reference to the validity of marriage, remain the same today as the time of Gratian. The great theologians and canonists, coming after Gratian's time merely took up the principles in regard to error of person and quality, laid down by the great Master and tried to make the principles clear by examples more appropriate than those used by Gratian himself. Notably among the great canonists and theologians before the Code, who have treated thoroughly the theory of error invalidating matrimonial consent may be cited Sanchez [83] who gives in regard to this question, many practical examples, Reiffenstuel and Schmalzgrueber,[84] both noted for their great clarity in treating the most difficult phases of this abstract question of error. Closer to our own day, Wernz and

[82] "Privatus enim error nec anteponi debet nec praejudicium offerre potest generali, quam, diximus, voluntati, ex qua contracti matrimonii validitas, et perpetuitas pendet."—Benedict XIV, *De Synod. dioec.*, lib. XIII, cap. 22, n. 3.

[83] Sanchez, *De Matrim.*, VII, disp. 18, nn. 1-15.

[84] Schmalzgrueber, *Jus Eccl. Univ.*, tit. IV, tit. 1, n. 440 sq.; Reiffenstuel, *Jus Canon. Univ.*, lib. IV, tit. 1, n. 325, sq.

Cardinal Gasparri [85] have also written invaluable treatises on error in their great works on Matrimony. The present Code, in its treatment of error invalidating matrimonial consent, simply embodies in the Code the same principles that have been taught by canonists and theologians for centuries before. However, the Code ceases to recognize error as an impediment to marriage and now places it among those defects which refer to matrimonial consent. Nevertheless, the doctrine of error remains essentially the same as in the time of Benedict XIV.

Article V—Roman Law

In Roman Law there is not found any reference to error of person and quality in regard to matrimonial consent.[86] However, there are found many principles that refer to consent in general and also to error in regard to contracts.

Very much attention is given in Roman Law to consent in reference to contracts because consent is always an essential element of a contract. For, since every contract in Roman Law is a *pactum,* either formal or non-formal, there must be an accord of wills which a *pactum* thus implies. For, whether this *pactum* is an unilateral contract in which only one obliges himself or whether the *pactum* is binding on both parties, there is demanded a reciprocal consent, or the accord of wills of those who are making the *pactum*.[87]

Hence, in Roman Law, where consent does not exist there can be no existing contract. For where consent is lacking, instead of an accord of wills that a contract implies, there is a

[85] Wernz, *Jus Canon.,* V, n. 463, sq.; Gasparri, *De Matrim,* n. 887, sq.

[86] Das römische Recht, welches wohl viele Bestimmungen für den Irrtum über persönliche Eigenschaften beim Sklavenkaufe enthalt, sagt nichts über den Irrtum bei der Eheschliessung. Hatten die Eheleute sich in persönlichen Eigenschaften geirrt, so machte das Recht ihnen die Ehescheidung sehr leicht."—Linneborn, *Grundrisz des Eherechts,* p. 272.

[87] Girard, *Manuel Eelementaire De Droit Romain,* p. 479; Ferrini, *Manuele Di Pandette,* n. 166.

situation existing where one wishes to bind himself, while the other does not wish to bind himself. Hence as there does not exist a harmony of wills the contract is invalid.[88]

Notably among the defects that destroy consent which is necessary for a true contract in Roman Law, is error.[89] Error is very frequently treated in the sources of Roman Law. Several texts are found in the sources which illustrate how error destroys consent.[90]

Error in Roman Law consists in this, that consent has been given, while one of the parties assumes that certain facts exist and these facts are not as they are assumed. In other words, consent due to this false assumption or error was not given to the facts, as they really exist, but only to those facts that were assumed. Hence, whenever error affected substantially the contract in Roman Law, it did so on the grounds that consent or agreement was lacking.[91] However, just when error did affect the contract to such an extent that the contract was rendered void, is difficult to ascertain from the sources.[92]

Authors, however, are accustomed to give three great classes in which error excludes consent and hence, makes the very contract invalid in Roman Law.

First, there is error *in negotio*. Error of the nature of the contract is only possible in contracts which are not formal. In such an error, one of the parties has wished to make one kind of an act and the other party a different act. For instance, one of the parties wishes to make a deposit and the other a *mutuum*. In this case, there is neither *mutuum* nor deposit,

[88] Buckland, *A Text-Book of Roman Law*, p. 412.

[89] Ferrini, *Manuele Di Pandette*, n. 167.

[90] "Non videntur, qui errant, consentire," L. 116 § 2 D. de div. reg. jur. antiqui 50, 17; "Nullus errantis consensus,"—L. 9. C. I, 18; "Nulla enim voluntas errantis est," L. 20. D. 39, 3.

[91] Girard, *Manuel Elementaire De Droit Romain*, p. 479.

[92] Buckland, *A Text-Book of Roman Law*, p. 412.

due to the error, which was made relative to the very nature of the contract that was entered into.[93]

The second kind of error is in regard to person. The classical law considered such an error of the identity of the person as if there had really been default of consent and hence, as a result, there could be no true contract. If, then, in Roman Law, one wished to lend money to a certain party whom he believes to be somebody else, the contract of *mutuum* is not formed. Error of quality of the person in this matter is of no importance.[94]

The last kind of error is error *in corpore*. This error occurs in regard to the very object of the contract itself so that there is lacking an equal accord of wills and hence, the existence of the contract is rendered impossible. Thus, when one sells silver for gold one of the contracting parties had given consent to buy gold and not the silver. The same error occurs when one slave is promised by a verbal contract and another is given in his place. The error has been essentially made in regard to the very object of the contract and two wills agreeing precisely on the same object do not exist and as an accord of wills is necessary for the validity of the contract the contract is necessarily rendered invalid.[95]

[93] Up. D. 12, 1.

[94] Paulus, D. 18, 2 *De in diem add.* 14, 3; Girard, *Manuel Élementaire De Droit Romain,* p. 480.

[95] Girard, *Manuel Élementaire De Droit Romain,* p. 480; Buckland, *A Text-Book of Roman Law,* p. 412; Ferrini, *Manuele Di Pandette,* n. 168.

CHAPTER II

DEFINITION AND DIVISION OF ERROR

MARRIAGE, by its very nature, is a solemn contract, entered into by two qualified persons giving to each other the right of their bodies for acts, placed for the generation of offspring. As in all other contracts, marriage is regulated by certain laws that must be adhered to, in order to insure its validity. One of the conditions demanded that marriage be a true contract is, that the consent given by both parties be a true consent and that nothing interfere to vitiate this consent. Among the various causes that may destroy the consent of the marriage contract is error which, under certain conditions, renders the contract null.[1]

Error in general [2] may be considered as a false apprehension of a thing. Error is distinct from ignorance. Ignorance is a lack of knowledge, but in the case of error, there is knowledge present but a wrong judgment has been given by the intellect.[3]

Applying the principles of error in general to matrimonial consent, it may be said, that error is a false judgment, at least on the part of one of the contracting parties, concerning the object to which matrimonial consent is given; namely one or both of the contracting parties, err in regard to the substance,

[1] C. 1083, 1084.

[2] Wernz-Vidal, *Jus Matrimonium,* V, n. 464; Chelodi, *Jus Matrim.,* n. III; Cappello, *De Sacram.,* III, n. 583; Ayrinhac, *Marriage Legislation in the New Code,* n. 192.

[3] Wernz-Vidal, *Jus Matrimonium,* V, n. 464; Chelodi, *Jus Matrim.,* n. 112; Cappello, *De Sacram.,* III, n. 583; Ayrinhac, *Marriage Legislation in the New Code,* n. 192.

or in regard to some of its qualities, so that it is something different than the intellect represents and the will seeks.[4]

Error in regard to matrimonial consent, may be of law or fact.[5] Error of law is of the nature or object of the marriage contract; it may also be of some essential property of marriage as for example, its unity, indissolubility or sacramental dignity.[6] Error of fact may be of the very person with whom one contracts marriage, or of some quality of this person.[7] Error may also be antecedent and concomitant. Antecedent error gives cause for the contract so that the contract is entered into on account of this error. If this error had not existed, the contract would not have been made.[8] Concomitant error does not give cause for the contract so that even if the party were aware of the error at the time of the marriage, the marriage would have still been contracted.[9]

[4] Gasparri, *De Matrim.,* n. 888; Cerato, *Matrim.,* n. 79, Farrugia, *De Matrim.,* n. 25; De Smet, *De Spons. et Matrim.,* n. 523.

[5] Wernz-Vidal, *Jus Matrim.,* n. 465; Blat, *Comment* III, pars, I, n. 482; Feije, *De Imped. et Disp. Matrim.,* n. 67.

[6] Payen, *De Matrim.,* III, n. 1626; Ayrinhac, *Marriage Legislation in the New Code of Canon Law,* 193; Tanquerey, *Synops. Theol. Moral.,* I, n. 717.

[7] Gasparri, *De Matrim.,* n. 888; Wernz-Vidal, *Jus Matrim.,* n. 465; De Smet, *De Spons. et Matrim.,* n. 523.

[8] Payen, *De Matrim.,* III, n. 1626; Ayrinhac, *Marriage Legislation in the New Code of Canon Law,* p. 193; Chelodi, *Jus Matrim.,* n. 112.

[9] Wernz-Vidal, *Jus Matrimonium,* V, n. 464; Cappello, *De Sacram,* III, n. 583; Payen, *De Matrim.,* III, n. 1626.

CHAPTER III

ERROR OF PERSON AND QUALITY

CANON 1083

1. **Error circa personam invalidum reddit matrimonium.**
2. **Error circa qualitatem personae, etsi det causam contractui, matrimonium irritat tantum:**
   1° Si error qualitatis redundet in errorem personae;
   2° Si persona libera matrimonium contrahat cum persona quam liberam putat, cum contra sit serva servitute proprie dicta.

ARTICLE I—ERROR OF PERSON

THE first paragraph of canon 1083, states that error of person renders marriage invalid. This error of person has been called substantial because it affects the very substance of the marriage contract.[1] The two persons giving their marital consent to each other are the substance of the matrimonial contract and hence, any error of person must be also error of the substance of the matrimonial contract.[2] Authors all agree that this error renders marriage invalid by natural law because the very nature of the marriage contract demands that two certain and definite persons give consent to each other at the moment of marriage.[3] But in the case of error of person, one of the parties

[1] C. 1083.

[2] Wernz-Vidal, *Jus Canon.*, V, n. 467; Cappello, *De Sacram.*, III, n. 584; Gasparri, *De Matrim.*, n. 887; Cerato, *Matrim.*, n. 79; Chelodi, *Jus Matrim.*, n. 112; Vlaming, *Praelect.*, n. 526.

[3] Farrugia, *De Matrim.*, n. 25; Gasparri, *De Matrim.*, n. 887; De Becker, *De Spons. et Matrim.*, p. 54; De Smet, *De Spons. et Matrim.*, n. 525; Chelodi, *Jus Matrim.*, n. 112.

does not give a true matrimonial consent at the time of the marriage. Thus A wishing to marry B, gives consent at the time of the marriage to C who is present and whom A wrongly believes to be B. Hence, there is here no mutual consent. The marriage of Jacob and Lia furnishes a very good example of this error of person.[4] Jacob, according to the Scriptural narrative, had requested in marriage and had been promised, his cousin Rachel but at the time of the marriage, his father-in-law substituted for Rachel, his first born daughter Lia. Jacob, not suspecting such a fraud, gave his consent to Lia whom he falsely believed to be Rachel. Thus the marriage was invalid.

However, apart from the marriage of a blind man or a marriage performed at night, as in the case of the marriage of Jacob and Lia, or a marriage by proxy, this error of person can scarcely happen.[5] It is not, however, beyond the realm of possibility. Fourneret thus presents this case which might very well happen.[6] A young man, in his youth, set out from France to the United States where he subsequently marries and has a son. All during his stay in America, this man has been in correspondence with a friend in Paris who has also married and has a daughter. It is the mutual wish of these two friends that their families be united in marriage and hence, the young couple, though they have never seen each other, thus agree to marry. On the day of the marriage an adventurer presents himself as the young American whom the young woman has agreed to marry. The father and the young girl have only known the intended bridegroom by reputation and so they are easily deceived by the fraud. The young woman then at the time of the marriage, wishes to marry the son of her father's friend and believing the man present to be the in-

[4] Genesis, 29:16-28.

[5] Cerato, *Matrim.*, n. 79; Gasparri, *De Matrim.*, n. 888; Farrugia, *De Matrim.*, n. 25; Cappello, *De Sacram.*, III, 585; Esmein, *Le Marriage en Droit Canonique*, I, 346; Noldin, *De Sacram.*, III, p. 638.

[6] Fourneret, *Le Mariage Chrétien*, p. 122.

tended spouse, proceeds to contract marriage. This marriage is evidently invalid because the young woman believes that she is giving her consent to the son of her father's friend, where as in reality, this man is not present at the moment of the marriage.[7]

It would be well to present here some practical rules, laid down by Cardinal Gasparri, in his work *De Matrimonio,* in reference to error of person. With the exception of a marriage of a blind man and such a marriage as that of Jacob and Lia, says this eminent author, in order that error of person occur, it is necessary that one of the parties wishes to marry a certain and definite person; that this person be unknown personally and that at the time of the marriage, another falsely represent himself or herself as the intended spouse.[8] The above example of Fourneret thus very well exemplifies this rule, for the young French girl wishes to marry a definite and determined person, who, however, was unknown to her personally. Moreover, at the time of the marriage, her intended bridegroom was absent while another fraudulently offered himself in his place.[9] If, however, the person knows the other party who falsely represents himself as the intended bridegroom, there is not error of person but only error of name, for in this case, it is presumed that the woman wished to marry the man present, that is, she wishes to give her consent to that man present before her. This presumption, however, yields to proof. If, on the contrary, the man who fraudulently offers himself as the intended spouse were unknown and also if there had been a previous arrangement for marriage, then it is presumed that the woman did not intend to marry the man present but rather

[7] Cappello, *De Sacram.,* III, n. 584; Tanquerey, *Synops. Theol. Moral.,* I, n. 717; Feije, *De Imped. et Disp. Matrim.,* n. 68; Blat, *Comment.,* III, pars I, n. 482; Noldin, *De Jure Matrim.,* n. 632.

[8] Gasparri, *De Matrim.,* n. 889.

[9] Fourneret, *Le Mariage Chrétien,* p. 122.

the absent man. The validity of the marriage, however, would be insured if the woman would say I wish to marry this man present whoever he may be. Her consent then would be truly given to the man present before her at the time of the marriage.[10]

Hence, error of person vitiates marriage by lack of consent because instead of giving consent to the person *hic et nunc* present the consent rather goes to a third and absent party.

It does not matter whether error of person is antecedent or concomitant.[11] Antecedent error would occur, if the erring party had known the error, he or she would never have contracted the marriage. In concomitant error, the erring party would have entered into the marriage, even if he were cognizant of the error. In regard to the former, it goes without saying that such an error would invalidate the marriage. As for concomitant error, Chelodi [12] points out, that such an error is hypothetical and not real, for it is not a question what the erring party would have done had he been cognizant of the error at the time of the marriage, but what he really did do at that particular time. Matrimonial consent is something actual and practical, given to the person present and if this consent is lacking, the marriage is invalid from the beginning.[13]

It also does not matter in regard to substantial error of person if this error has been induced by fraud or by inadvert-

[10] Gasparri, *De Matrim.*, n. 889; Farrugia, *De Matrim.*, n. 25; Blat, *Comment.*, III, pars I, n. 482; Bevilacqua, *Matrim.*, 376; Cance, *Droit Çanonique*, n. 312.

[11] Feije, *De Imped. et Desp. Matrim.*, n. 68; Bangen, *Instruc. Pract. De Spons. et Matrim.*, n. 82; Schmalzgrueber, *Jus Eccles. Univ.*, lib. IV, tit. 1, n. 440; Rosset, *De Matrim.*, n. 1228; De Becker, *De Spons. et Matrim.*, p. 55; De Smet, *De Spons. et Matrim.*, n. 525.

[12] Chelodi, *Jus Matrim.*, n. 112.

[13] Wernz-Vidal, *Jus Canon.*, V, n. 467; Chelodi, *Jus Matrim.*, n. 112; Lehmkul, *Theol. Moral.*, II, n. 734; D'Annibale, *Summula Moral.*, III, n. 444; Ayrinhac, *Marriage Legislation in the New Code*, n. 194.

ence of the erring party.[14] In both cases the marriage is invalid, because either due to the fraud or the inadvertence of the mistaken party, an erroneous judgment exists in the mind of one of the parties and as a result of this erroneous judgment, the consent has been given to a person other than the person present at the time of the marriage.[15]

Nor can it be objected that as long as the two parties cohabit together and carnal relations ensue the marriage becomes valid. For as long as the party in error has not become aware of the error, the marriage still remains invalid because consent alone makes the marriage valid and not the carnal copulation.[16]

Since then error of person most firmly rests upon the law of nature, it is easily seen that infidels, even if there exists no provision against error of person in the civil law, come under this most evident law of nature.[17] The fact that error of person was formerly placed among the impediments that vitiated marriage, merely affirmed this most evident natural law.[18]

Article II—Error of Quality in General

Error of quality, even though it is the cause of the contract, does not vitiate the matrimonial contract either by natural or positive law.[19] It does not vitiate consent by natural law be-

[14] Fourneret, *Le Mariage Chrétien,* p. 122; De Smet, *De Spons. et Matrim.,* n. 525; De Becker, *De Spons. et Matrim.,* p. 55.

[15] Feije, *De Imped. et Disp. Matrim.,* n. 70; Bangen, *Instruc. Pract. De Spons. et Matrim.,* p. 82.

[16] Cerato, *Matrim.,* n. 79; Ballerini-Palmieri, *Theol. Moral.,* VI, n. 603.

[17] Bevilacqua, *Matrim.,* n. 376; Wernz-Vidal, *Jus Canon.,* V, n. 467; Vlaming, *Praelect.,* n. 527; Rosse, *De Matrim.,* n. 1249; Cance, *Droit Canonique,* n. 312.

[18] Chelodi, *Jus Matrim.,* n. 112.

[19] Reiffenstuel, *Jus Canon. Univ.,* lib. IV, tit. 1, 345; Cappello, *De Sacram.,* III, n. 585; Sanchez, *Jus Matrim.,* VII, disp. 18, n. 11; Vermeersch-Creusen, *Epitome,* II, n. 370; De Smet, *De Spons. et Matrim.,* n. 525.

cause full consent of the will has been given to the object or substance of the contract, i.e., the will reaches out and grasps that object which the intellect proposes and although in the case of error of quality, the intellect is deceived by error, the intellect nevertheless proposes this object to the will absolutely and the will embraces the object absolutely. In other words, the substance (that is the person) of the contract is not deficient.[20]

As in error of person, this error of quality may be concomitant, antecedent, or it may be induced by fraud and the gravest damages may befall the one who is thus deceived. It is clear that concomitant error in regard to error of quality does not invalidate the marriage because the erring party would have married were he aware of the truth at the time of the marriage.[21] Nor does antecedent error affect the validity of the marriage even though the erring party would have abhorred before marriage the existence of such a quality and would have even expressed this horror to others before marriage.[22]

It must be pointed out here that fraud, even though it be induced by the other party and even though great damage thus accrues from it, does not destroy consent of the marriage.[23] In a case tried before the Sacred Congregation of the Council, the validity of a marriage was upheld even though a woman, rep-

[20] Chelodi, *Jus Matrim.*, n. 113; Tanquerey, *Synop. Theol. Moral.*, I, n. 719; Gasparri, *De Matrim.*, n. 892; D'Annibale, *Summula Moral.*, III, n. 444; Feije, *De Imped. et Disp. Matrim.*, n. 69.

[21] Vlaming, *Praelect.*, n. 527; De Becker, *De Spons.* et Matrim., p. 56; Cappello, *De Sacram.*, III, n. 585; Rosset, *De Matrim.*, n. 1249.

[22] Blat, *Comment.*, III, pars I, n. 482; Vlaming, *Praelect.*, n. 527; Farrugia, *De Matrim.*, n. 25; Cerato, *Matrim.*, n. 79; Noldin, *De Sacram.*, III, p. 638.

[23] Bangen, *Instruc. Pract. De Spons. et Matrim.*, p. 83; Lehmkul, *Theol. Moral.*, II, n. 733; Ballerini-Palmieri, *Theol. Moral.*, VI, n. 603; Augustine, *A Commentary on Canon Law*, V, 234; Reiffenstuel, *Jus Canon. Univ.*, lib. IV, tit. I, 345; Petrovits, *The New Church Law on Marriage*, n. 406.

resented herself as enceinte through the fault of a particular man, in order to induce this particular man to marry her. Although in this case, the man married the woman, believing and for the reason that he was the cause of the pregnancy, the Sacred Congregation of the Council held the marriage to be valid since the man had but erred due to the fraud of the woman in regard to a quality and had failed to make his consent depend upon the truth of the woman's statement.[24] Justice, however, requires that the damage be repaired in some way by that party who thus induced it, but the marriage remains valid.[25]

Nor is there given here a cause of recission as in other contracts.[26] First of all it is due to the fact, that marriage is not only a sacred contract but it is also one of the seven Sacraments instituted by Christ.[27] Furthermore, canon 104, which refers to causes of recission states clearly that it is only where there is substantial error, that there may exist a cause of recission. But here, in the case of error of quality, when it deals with the marriage contract, there is not substantial but merely accidental error since the consent of the erring party had been given absolutely to the object or person of the contract and although error is present in this particular contract, it is only in reference to a quality and not to the substance of the contract.[28]

[24] *AAS.*, II, p. 102.

[25] Where serious fraud has been perpetrated upon the innocent party, although the marriage remains valid, the injured party may seek a separation from bed, board and dwelling. Bevilacqua, *Matrim.*, n. 379; Cance, *Droit Canonique*, n. 312.

[26] Cappello, *De Sacram.*, III, n. 585; Chelodi, *Jus Matrim.*, n. 112; Farrugia, *De Matrim.*, n. 25; Bevilacqua, *Matrim.*, n. 380; Vlaming, *Praelect.*, n. 527.

[27] Blat., *Comment.*, III, pars I, n. 482; *Cerato, Matrim.*, n. 79.

[28] De Smet, *De Spons. et Matrim.*, n. 525; Chelodi, *Jus Matrim.*, n. 112; Cappello, *De Sacram.*, III, n. 585; Ayrinhac, *Marriage Legislation in the New Code*, n. 195; Bangen, *Instruc. Pract. De Spons. et Matrim.*, p. 83.

As a secondary proof that error of quality does not invalidate marriage, it may be stated that in all these cases the law presupposes that those entering marriage use that precaution that is naturally expected of people entering into such a sacred contract as marriage which is minding upon both parties until the death of one of the parties.[29] Not a few modern Civil Legislators have taken certain qualities as epilepsy or syphilis or some other qualities and have made error in regard to these qualities vitiate matrimonial consent.[30] However, the Church has never followed such example.[31] In this regard she has greatly shown her wisdom and her prudence, since such a legislation would lead to the annulment of innumerable marriages, others it would render doubtful while at the same time it would be the cause of much litigation.[32] For it is common experience that not a few men and women, after some years of married life, complain that if they had known that their wives or husbands had such or such a defect, at the time of the marriage, they would never have married them.[33]

Article III—Error of Quality Redounding to Error of Person

Canon 1083, after stating that error of quality does not render marriage null, proceeds to give two notable exceptions. The first is that when error of quality redounds to error of

[29] "Le Brocard un peu cynique de nos peres: 'En Mariage trompe qui peut, semble être en effect la regale de conduite d'un trop grand nombre de futurs epoux."—Fourneret, *Le Mariage Chrétien,* p. 121; Woywod, *A Practical Commentary on The Code of Canon Law,* I, n. 1081; De Smet, *De Spons. et Matrim.,* n. 525.

[30] Cappello, *De Sacram.,* III, n. 592; Wernz-Vidal, *Jus Canon.,* V, 467.

[31] Cappello, *De Sacram.,* III, n. 591; Wernz-Vidal, *Jus Canon.,* V, n. 469; Chelodi, *Jus Matrim.,* n. 112.

[32] Cerato, *Matrim.,* n. 79; Gasparri, *De Matrim.,* 896; Bermeerch-Creusen, *Epitome,* II, n. 370.

[33] Farrugia, *De Matrim.,* n. 25; Chelodi, *Jus Matrim.,* n. 113; Cappello, *De Sacram.,* III, n. 585; Bevilacqua, *Matrim.,* n. 379.

person, the marriage is null. In regard to this kind of error, Chelodi points out that even until recent times this question has not been rightly understood.[34] Hence, there have been confused declarations among authors and erroneous applications of judges. Clericatus also states "Verum ad cognoscendum, quando error redundet in substantiam personae, adeo confusi et discordes sunt Doctores in assignanda regula, ut illi, qui se profitentur faciliores, in effectu obscuriores evadent, et quod multi asserunt de nullitate matrimonii circa errorem qualitatis, alii affirmant de validitate."[35] There has been so great agitation in regard to this question in the past, that St. Alphonsus has referred to it as a great controversy.[36]

As pointed out in tracing the historical development of this particular error, canonists did not come to consider this error until very late,[37] and it was really St. Thomas who first formulated the terminology which is now used in regard to it.[38] Among the modern authors, Wernz [39] calls this error substantial by the very law of nature, Vlaming[40] says it is the one exception of quality given by the natural law, De Smet [41] calls it accidental, while Cappello[42] says that this error is really substantial since the quality is of such a nature that it is identical with the person and thus renders the marriage invalid.

A few principles may be set down here in order to judge whether error of quality redounds to error of person. First,

[34] Chelodi, *Jus Matrim.*, n. 112. Footnote 4.

[35] Clericatus, *De Matrim.*, Dec. 19, n. 27.

[36] St. Alphonsus, *Theol. Moral.*, VI, 1013.

[37] Esmein, *Le Mariage en Droit Canonique*, I, 346; Freisen, *Geschichte des Canonischen Eherechts*, 278; Wernz-Vidal, *Jus Canon*, V, n. 466.

[38] St. Thomas, *Summa Theol.*, p. III, Suppl. q. 51, art. I, ad 5; Esmein, *Le Mariage en Droit Canonique*, I, 346; Fourneret, *Le Mariage Chrétien*, p. 122.

[39] Wernz-Vidal, *Jus Canon.*, V, n. 468.

[40] Vlaming, *Praelect.*, n. 527.

[41] De Smet, *De Spons. et Matrim.*, n. 526.

[42] Cappello, *De Sacram.*, III, n. 586.

it should be determined whether the quality is of such a nature that the person is thus distinguished from every other person and hence, by this quality the person is so individualized, that the quality really stands for the person.[43] The classical example of this quality given by ancient authors and also by authors today, is that of being the first born child.[44] This quality is so distinctive that it really distinguishes its possessor from every other person. Hence, this quality may be said to stand for the person itself because, if error is made in regard to this quality, the error is consequently made in regard to the identity of the person also.[45] But this quality of being the first born child is not the only quality relative to which this error may be made. It is only necessary that there be error of a quality that thus fully determines and distinguishes its possessor from other persons.[46]

The second principle is, that the person is not known to the erring party unless by that quality in regard to which he errs or at least, this quality be the principle quality known to the party who thus errs. For unless this is true, then it may easily happen that the erring party be captivated by other qualities of the person whom he wishes to marry and hence these other qualities do not distinguish this particular person from other people.[47] In order to judge whether there has been error of quality redounding to error of person, it will be useful to know if the party who has erred in regard to this quality had known the party by hearsay or rumor before he became aware

[43] St. Alphonsus, *Theol. Moral.*, VI, n. 1015; Bangen, *Instruct. Pract. De Spons. et Matrim.*, p. 83; Gasparri, *De Matrim.*, n. 816; Cappello, *De Sacram.*, III, n. 586; Blat, *Comment.*, III, pars I, n. 482; Farrugia, *De Matrim.*, n. 25.

[44] Sanchez, *Jus Matrim.*, VII, disp. 18; Carriere, *Praelect., Theol. de Matrim.*, II, n. 635; St. Alphonsus, *Theol. Moral.*, VI, n. 1015; Cerato, *Matrim.*, n. 79; Cappello, *De Sacram.*, III, n. 586.

[45] Wernz-Vidal, *Jus Canon.*, V, n. 468.

[46] Bangen, *Instruc. Pract. De Spons. et Matrim.*, p. 84; Chelodi, *Jus Matrim.*, n. 112; Feije, *De Imped. et Disp. Matrim.*, n. 73.

[47] Bangen, *Instruc. Pract. De Spons. et Matrim.*, p. 84.

of the existence of such particular quality. It is also important to know whether the erring party had already determined to marry the person before he thus had an opportunity of meeting her, i.e., whether he had only known her from hearsay or only on the recommendation of others.[48] The reason for these simple observations is quite clear. If the person had been known by the erring party before the marriage, then there is great probability that his consent was given directly to the person known and not to a quality that really individualized the person.[49]

The third principle to be considered is, whether the intention directly and principally falls on the quality in regard to which the party errs, or whether it principally and directly falls on the person whom the erring party believes to possess such a quality. A simple example will tend to illustrate this point. If a certain man wishes to marry the first born child of a certain king or prince and he believes that the person present possesses this quality, then if this person present does not have this quality, there exists error of quality redounding to error of person.[50] Because the consent of the man is given to the quality and the quality is such as to be equivalent to the person itself and hence, in this case, error of quality is the same as error of person.[51] But on the contrary, if the same man wishes to marry the person present whom he believes to be the first born child of a certain king or prince, then even though this quality is lacking, there is present a true and valid

[48] Gasparri, *De Matrim.*, n. 899; Feije, *De Imped. et Disp. Matrim.*, n. 73; Bangen, *Instruc. Pract. De Spons. et Matrim.*, p. 84.

[49] St. Alphonsus, *Theol. Moral.*, VI, n. 1015; Blat, *Comment.*, III, pars I, n. 482; Vlaming, *Praelect.*, n. 527.

[50] Sanchez, *Jus Matrim.*, VII, disp. 18, n. 35; Schmalzgrueber, *Jus Eccles. Univ.*, IV, tit. n. 448; Bangen, *Instruc. Pract. De Spons. et Matrim.*, p. 85; Gasparri, *De Matrim.*, n. 896; Ballerini-Palmieri, *Theol. Moral.*, VI, n. 604.

[51] Wernz-Vidal, *Jus Canon.*, V, n. 465; Blat, *Comment.*, III, pars I, n. 482; Vlaming, *Praelect.*, n. 527; Vermeerch-Creusen, *Epitome*, II, n. 370; Bevilacqua, *Matrim.*, n. 379.

marriage, for in this case, the erring person thus gives consent truly to the person before him and only errs in regard to a quality which is only accidental and does not redound to error of person.

Hence, it may be said that as long as there is not a question of a quality which does not determine and individualize the person, or as long as there is not a quality which alone is known in regard to the person and as long as the erring party does not directly and chiefly intend this quality, error in regard to a quality does not invalidate a marriage.[52] It is evident then that such qualities as virginity or wealth do not determine and individualize the person who possesses them, since there are many in the world who possess these qualities, and hence, error relative to these qualities does not invalidate a marriage.[53] On the contrary, if there is a question of a quality that truly determines the person and such a quality is intended then there is error of quality redounding to error of person.[54]

In practice it may be stated that there is scarcely ever occasion for error of quality redounding to error of person and what at first sight seems to be this error, on closer study turns out to be a question of quality to which a condition has been placed.[55]

[52] Feije, *De Imped. et Disp. Matrim.*, n. 73; Lehmkul, *Theol. Moral.*, II, n. 734; De Becker, *De Spons. et Matrim.*, p. 56; Rosset, *De Matrim.*, n. 1261.

[53] Chelodi, *Jus Matrim.*, n. 112; Farrugia, *De Matrim.*, n. 25; Cerato, *Matrim.*, n. 79.

[54] St. Thomas, *Summa Theol.*, pars III, Suppl. q. 51, art. I ad 5; De Smet, *De Spons. et Matrim.*, n. 526; D'Annibale, *Summula Moral.*, III, n. 444; Cappello, *De Sacram.*, III, n. 586.

[55] Bangen, *Instruc. Pract. De Spons. et Matrim.*, p. 87; De Becker, *De Spons. et Matrim.*, p. 56; Feije, *De Imped. et Disp. Matrim.*, n. 73; Blat, *Comment.*, III, pars I, n. 482; n. 896; Bevilacqua, *Matrim.*, n. 379.

Article IV—Error of Servitude

Error of servitude formerly was placed among those impediments that vitiated matrimonial consent, now it is placed among those defects of consent that render marriage invalid.[56] As has been pointed out previously, this error today has very little practical importance in the Church save in those countries where slavery still exists, i.e., chiefly in missionary countries. The legislation in regard to this canon remains identically the same as that which existed before the Code. Just as in the former legislation, three things must exist in the present law in order that such an error of servile condition render the marriage invalid. First, one of the parties must be a slave in the true sense of the word, secondly, one of the parties of the marriage must be a free person and not a slave, and finally, the free party must be ignorant at the time of the marriage of the servile condition of the other party.[57]

The question arises here whether error of servile condition thus invalidating marriage, rests upon the legislation of the Church solely [58] or upon natural law.[59] Most authors claim that error of servile condition is based upon ecclesiastical law alone.[60] The reasons given by the majority of canonists and theologians that this error rests only upon the legislation of the Church may be thus briefly summed up. Although a slave has the inherent right to marry and has even a right to marry a free party, yet there is so natural repugnance in free people,

[56] C. 1083.

[57] Cappello, *De Sacram.*, III, n. 586; Vermeersch-Creusen, *Epitome*, II, n. 370; Noldin, *De Sacram.*, III, p. 638; De Smet, *De Spons. et Matrim.*, n. 526; Wernz-Vidal, *Jus Canon.*, V, n. 479; Gasparri, *De Matrim.*, n. 903; Rosset, *De Matrim.*, n. 1522.

[58] Wernz-Vidal, *Jus Canon.*, V, n. 479; Chelodi, *Jus Matrim.*, n. 112; Cappello, *De Sacram.*, III, n. 586; Ayrinhac, *Marriage Legislation in the New Code*, n. 195; Bangen, *Instruc. Pract. De Spons. et Matrim.*, p. 70.

[59] Cerato, *Matrim.*, n. 79.

[60] Farrugia, *De Matrim.*, n. 25.

towards slavery, that the Church is unwilling to subject a Catholic party to such a marriage as long as he or she is ignorant of the condition of the servile party before the marriage was entered into.[61] Furthermore, there does not only exist this natural repugnance to slavery on the part of free people but by the mere fact that the slave is subject absolutely to the will of the master there is grave danger that the marital rights of the free party may thus be seriously interfered with and the children of such a union be in peril of being denied the opportunity of receiving a Catholic education and practicing their religion.[62] However, if the free party realizes the condition of the slave and yet wishes to marry, he is to be considered as willing to take upon himself all the inconveniences and discomforts that such a union may have for him.[63]

In order that error of servitude invalidate a marriage, the first condition is, that one of the persons be a slave in the proper sense of the word. Here the word slave or *servus* must be taken in that sense as is understood in Roman Law; namely, a man or woman must be absolutely under the power of another, so that he or she can be bought or sold at the will of the master.[64] Hence, the word *servus* here is taken in a different meaning than that of servant, i.e., those who for small wages do menial work for others.[65] Nor are those considered under the name *servus* who are perpetually bound to a certain piece of land or who while laboring for others are allowed to retain from the fruit of their work only those things that are

[61] Gasparri, *De Matrim.*, n. 903; Cappello, *De Sacram.*, III, n. 586; Lehmkule, *Theol. Moral.*, II, n. 733; Vlaming, *Praelect.*, II, n. 527; Wernz-Vidal, *Jus Canon.*, V, n. 479.

[62] Noldin, *De Sacram.*, III, p. 638; Chelodi, *Jus Matrim.*, n. 112; Blat, *Comment.*, III, pars I, n. 482.

[63] Cappello, *De Sacram.*, III, n. 586; Farrugia, *De Matrim.*, n. 25; Feije, *De Imped. et Disp. Matrim.*, n. 72.

[64] Cappello, *De Sacram.*, III, n. 586; Chelodi, *Jus Matrim.*, n. 112.

[65] Farrugia, *De Matrim.*, n. 25; Vlaming, *Praelect.*, n. 527.

absolutely essential for the maintenance of their lives.[66] Only those who are entirely under the dominion of another are considered under the word *servus* as used in this canon.

The second condition is, that one of the parties be free at the time of the contracted marriage.[67] It does not matter whether the party who now is free was formerly a slave, the only thing required is, that he be free at the time of the marriage. If on the contrary, a slave marries another slave with the mistaken idea that he is free, this error does not affect the validity of the marriage.[68]

The third condition that must be kept in mind in regard to error of servitude is this, that the free party must be ignorant of the servile condition of the other party at the time of the marriage,[69] other wise, if the party knew of the existing servitude and at the same time freely contracted marriage, then, he or she must be considered as consenting to the conditions rendered necessary by the servile condition of his or her spouse.

Hence, whenever these three conditions exist, this error of servile condition invalidates marriage. It makes no difference, whether this error is antecedent or concomitant, vincible or invincible, the result is always the same.[70] Since, however, this legislation rests solely upon the law of the Church, those unbaptised do not come under the prescription of this canon.[71] If, however, the baptised party is free and the unbaptised party

[66] Blat, *Comment.*, III, pars I, n. 482; Wernz-Vidal, *Jus Canon.*, V, n. 478.

[67] Cerato, *Matrim.*, n. 79; Ballerini-Palmieri, *Theol. Moral.*, VI, n. 613.

[68] Chelodi, *Jus Matrim.*, n. 112; Blat, *Comment.*, III, pars I, n. 482; Noldin, *De Sacram.*, III, p. 638.

[69] Cerato, *Matrim.*, n. 79; De Smet, *De Spons. et Matrim.*, n. 526; Feije, *De Imped. et Disp. Matrim.*, n. 72.

[70] Wernz-Vidal, *Jus Canon.*, V, n. 479; Vermeersch-Creusen, *Epitome*, II, n. 370; Cappello, *De Sacram.*, III, n. 586.

[71] Chelodi, *Jus Matrim.*, n. 112; Cappello, *De Sacram.*, III, n. 586; Cerato, *Matrim.*, n. 79.

a slave, this legislation in regard to error of servile condition would apply, but not vice versa.[72]

Some authors have maintained that marriage is valid from the moment it was celebrated, notwithstanding the existing error, if the slave becomes free within six months after the marriage.[73] However, this opinion does not seem to rest upon firm ground, since the law of the Church in regard to this error renders the marriage null absolutely, at the time it was entered into, and hence, once the liberty of the slave has been obtained, the marriage still remains null, unless a new matrimonial consent has been given.[74] However, if the slave obtains freedom by the very fact that he or she marries, the marriage is valid from the beginning [75] even though the free party were not aware of his or her servile condition before the time of the marriage. The law only demands that one of the parties of the marriage be in slavery at the time of the marriage, but in the above case, the slave receives her freedom when the marriage is performed.

If a free party then has contracted marriage with a slave whose servile condition has been unknown to him, before the marriage, such a party has a right to ask that the marriage be annulled, even though carnal copulation has ensued before the free party has become aware of the servile condition of the other party.

St. Alphonsus holds as probable, that in the case where a slave in good faith and entirely devoid of fraud, marries a

[72] Gasparri, *De Matrim.*, n. 904; De Smet, *De Spons. et Matrim.*, n. 526; Wernz-Vidal, *Jus Canon.*, V, n. 480.

[73] Sanchez, *Jus Matrim.*, VII, disp. 18, n. 13; Schmalzgrueber, *Jus Eccles.*, IV, tit. I, n. 36; St. Alphonsus, *Theol. Moral.*, VII, n. 1023.

[74] Cappello, *De Sacram.*, III, n. 586; Feije, *De Imped. et Disp. Matrim.*, n. 72; Wernz-Vidal, *Jus Canon.*, n. 247.

[75] Sanchez, *Jus Matrim.*, VII, disp. 20, n. 12; Gasparri, *De Matrim.*, n. 904; Ballerini-Palmieri, *Theol. Moral.*, VI, n. 612; Cappello, *De Sacram.*, III, n. 586.

free person, who is ignorant of the servile condition of his spouse such a slave is able to ask that the marriage be annulled. Cappello goes yet further and maintains that it is not only probable but entirely certain that a slave, in such circumstances is able to ask for annulment, because the marriage has not yet been sealed and as it is null for both parties, the slave has as equal a right as the free party, to ask for annulment.[76]

Not only did the ancient civil laws prohibit marriage between a free party and a slave, but in some cases, they even prohibited a marriage between free people of different ranks of society and citizens, violating such laws, were often severely punished. Thus the Roman citizens were not allowed to contract marriage with barbarians, nor was a Roman woman of a senatorial family permitted to marry one who was not of her social position in life.[77]

Although today, among civilized people, there is very little distinction made between various ranks of society, in regard to marriage, yet in some countries, there is seen a vestige of these ancient laws. Hence, in some countries still, there is to be found what is called a morganatic marriage which in some respect, is based upon such ancient civil laws. Hence, those of the ruling house in some countries, are not allowed to marry "plene" except with those who are of royal blood. In such a union, the children born assume the social position and name of that parent who is of the lower rank in society. However, the Church is not opposed to such marriages and, provided they have been validly and licitly entered into, the Church recognizes these marriages as true marriages and considers the children born of them as legitimate. The Church has always been opposed to such class distinctions in regard to

[76] Cappello, *De Sacram.*, III, n. 586; St. Alphonsus, *Theol. Moral.*, VII, n. 1020.

[77] L XXIII, D. 2 *de rit. nupt.*

the Sacrament of Matrimony, because such class distinction is little in accord with the teachings of the Church which recognizes all her children as members of one great Christian family.[78]

In the Decretals, while treating of this question of servile condition, the marriage of lepers was considered and it was asked whether the legislation of error of servile condition, would also apply to leprosy or any other horrible and similar disease which is perpetual and scarcely curable. These diseases may be antecedent or occur after the marriage has been entered into. If the disease has been contracted before the marriage, it may thus render the marriage useless. In regard to such diseases, no matter how horrible they may be, or how useless they may render the marriage, the universal Church has always held that such marriages are valid. If the disease should occur after the marriage and there is grave danger of being afflicted, a separation *quoad thorum* may be sought. If the marriage has not been consummated, there may also be applied for, a dispensation *super ratum*. But if the marriage is thus dissolved, it is done so not on account of leprosy but on the grounds of *ratum non consummatum*.[79]

[78] Wernz-Vidal, *Jus Canon.*, V, n. 486; Schmalzgrueber, *Jus Eccl. Univ.*, IV, t. 1, n. 237.

[79] Wernz-Vidal, *Jus Canon.*, V, n. 489.

CHAPTER IV

SIMPLE ERROR

Canon 1084

Simplex error circa Matrimonii unitatem vel indissolubilitatem aut sacramentalem dignitatem, etsi det causam contractui, non vitiat consensum matrimonialem.

This canon points out that simple error in regard to the unity or indissolubility or sacramental dignity of marriage, even though it is the cause of the matrimonial contract, does not vitiate matrimonial consent.[1] This error is called simple because it remains in the intellect and does not influence the will of the contracting party in any way.[2] Hence, the error consists in this, that one or both of the contracting parties falsely think or believe at the time of the marriage that a true and lawful marriage may be dissolved, especially on account of the adultery of one of the parties and that another lawful marriage may be entered into, while the parties of the first marriage are still living; or one or both of the contracting parties may falsely believe that it is lawful to have several wives or husbands at the same time, as the Mohammedans falsely believe today, or they may even deny the sacramental dignity of marriage as most Protestants at present do.[3] But

[1] C. 1084.

[2] Blat, *Comment.*, III, pars I, n. 483; Cappello, *De Sacram.*, III, n. 588; Gasparri, *De Matrim.*, n. 901; De Becker, *De Spons. et Matrim.*, p. 57; Wernz-Vidal, *Jus Canon.*, V, n. 491.

[3] Benedictus XIV, *De Synodo Dioec.*, XIII, c. 22, n. 2; D'Annibale, *Summula Moral.*, III, n. 444; Gasparri, *De Matrim.*, n. 903; Farrugia, *De Matrim.*, n. 28; Lehmkuhl, *Theol. Moral.*, II, 734; Ballerini-Palmieri, *Theol. Moral.*, V, n. 602; Augustine, *A Commentary on Canon Law*, V, 235.

as long as this error remains in the intellect, and does not affect in any way the consent of the will at the time of the marriage, the marriage remains valid. There is nothing incompatible in the fact of simple error existing at the same time with a true and valid consent of the contracting party to the substance of the matrimonial contract.[4]

The reason why simple error does not vitiate matrimonial consent is due to the fact that one or both of the contracting parties, at the time of the marriage, do not exclude by a positive act of will one of the essential properties of marriage.[5] Marriage has been endowed by God with certain properties and it is entirely beyond the ability of man to separate these properties from the matrimonial contract.[6] However, men may falsely believe that they can separate one of the essential properties of marriage and still marry validly as is evident in the case of heretics who believe in divorce, and in the case of Mohammedans who sanction a plurality of wives. These men may even proceed to violate one of the essential properties of marriage after the marriage has been entered into. But although they may thus err and even contract marriage in such an error, as long as they simply believe or think that one or both of the essential properties can be separated from marriage, and as long as this belief does not affect in any way their will, there exists a true and valid marriage.[7]

[4] Chelodi, *Jus Matrim.*, n. 113; Cerato, *Matrim.*, n. 80; Vlaming, *Praelect.*, n. 529; De Smet, *De Spons. et Matrim.*, n. 529; Vermeersch-Creusen, *Epitome*, II, n. 371.

[5] Cappello, *De Sacram.*, III, n. 588; Gasparri, *De Matrim.*, n. 903; Blat, *Comment.*, III, pars I, n. 483; Reiffenstuel, *Jus Canon. Univ.*, lib. IV, t. I, n. 350; St. Alphonsus, *Theol. Moral.*, VII, n. 1019; Tanquerey, *Synops. Theol. Moral.*, I, n. 717; Noldin, *De Sacram.*, III, n. 632.

[6] Wernz-Vidal, *Jus Canon.*, V, n. 492; De Smet, *De Spons. et Matrim.*, n. 529; Perrone, *De Matrim.*, II, n. 509; Rosset, *De Matrim.*, n. 1268; Vlaming, *Praelect.*, n. 529.

[7] Benedictus XIV, *De Synodo Dioec.*, XIII, c. 22, n. 2; St. Thomas, *Summa*, pars. III, q. LI, art. 2; Farrugia, *De Matrim.*, n. 28; Chelodi, *Jus*

Benedict XIV, the classical authority on this difficult question, thus explains how such people, be they heretics, Pagans, Jews or Schismatics, laboring under the influence of this kind of error may, notwithstanding their error, thus contract a true marriage. Nearly all heretics and schismatics, says this learned author, when they marry, desire to enter into marriage according to the mind of Christ, and most Pagans when they marry, wish to marry in accord with the laws of nature. However, while such men and women wish to marry according to the mind of Christ, or according to nature's law, they may easily fall into the error that divorce is legitimate or as is the case with Mohammedans today, think there is nothing wrong in having at the same time, two or more wives. But as long as these contracting parties thus laboring under such a pernicious error have a general intention of contracting marriage, according to the mind of Christ or according to the laws of nature, then their general intention absorbs their particular error.[8] Hence, the reason why so many heretics, Greek Schismatics and Pagans contract valid marriages, even though they have contracted marriage in such error.[9]

Thus it has always been the practice of the Church, and this practice has now been made law, to consider all such marriages as valid, until it has been proved, in the external forum that one or both of the parties excluded by a positive act of the will one of the essential properties of marriage, at the time, when they contracted marriage.[10] Nor does it matter, as the canon points out, whether this error is the cause of the contract, that is to say, that the party who thus labors

Matrim., n. 113; Petrovits, *The New Church Law on Marriage,* n. 408; Bevilacqua, *Matrim.*, n. 387.

[8] Benedictus XIV, *De Synodo Dioec.*, XII, c. 22, n. 2.

[9] Chelodi, *Jus Matrim.*, n. 113; Cerato, *Matrim.*, n. 80; Ayrinhac, *Marriage Legislation in the New Code,* n. 198.

[10] Wernz-Vidal, *Jus Canon.*, V, n. 492; Vermeerch-Creusen, *Epitome,* II, n. 371; Vlaming, *Praelect.*, n. 529.

under this error would not have contracted the marriage were he aware of the truth, or if he realized the truth at the time of the marriage and still contracted marriage, he would have excluded one of the essential properties of marriage.[11] For it cannot be doubted that many heretics or schismatics, if they had been questioned, before they had contracted marriage, concerning the indissolubility of marriage or if they had adverted to the fact, would either have not married or would have excluded one of the properties that are essential to marriage.[12] But since at the moment of marriage under the influence of this error they did not exclude by a positive act of the will, one of the essential properties of marriage, the marriage is valid for it is not a question what a man would have done, but what he actually did at the time of the marriage. Common experience shows that many men, later in life looking back upon some particular action of their earlier life, now that they are better informed or realize the truth, would act quite differently now than they had acted on a particular former occasion. But it is clear that their past action is not to be judged in the light of their present state of mind but on the contrary, according to their state of mind when *de facto* they made such an action in the past.[13]

On the contrary, if under the influence of error or in the presence of error, one or both of the contracting parties by a positive act of the will, exclude from their consent one of the essential properties of marriage, i.e., the unity or indissolubility of marriage, then certainly the marriage is invalid.[14] For then

[11] C. 1084.

[12] Benedictus XIV, *De Synodo Dioec.*, XIII, c. 22, n. 2; Gasparri, *De Matrim.*, n. 903; Blat, *Comment.*, III, pars I, n. 483; Farrugia, *De Matrim.*, n. 28.

[13] Bevilacqua, *Matrim.*, n. 387; Fourneret, *Le Mariage Chrétien*, p. 124; Cappello, *De Sacram.*, III, n. 588; De Smet, *De Spons. et Matrim.*, n. 529; De Becker, *De Spons. et Matrim.*, p. 57.

[14] Wernz-Vidal, *Jus Canon.*, V, n. 492; Gasparri, *De Matrim.*, n. 903;

the error remains no longer simple error, that is to say, solely terminated by the intellect, but it thus affects the will of the contracting parties or party, so that they not only think for instance that the matrimonial bond is dissoluble, but under the influence of this error, they even proceed to exclude this essential property of indissolubility from their consent. The same holds true, even if the contracting party or parties, positively and expressly wish to contract a true marriage, but at the same time desire and are determined not to have an indissoluble marriage; the marriage is null from the beginning.[15] Hence, the contracting party does not thus give his consent absolutely to the substance of the matrimonial contract because he has at the time of the marriage, a positive will essentially contrary to the marriage itself. Whereas, in the case of simple error, the contracting party, even though in error, gives his consent absolutely to the substance of the marriage and thus implicity accepts the properties of marriage.[16]

The presumption, however, is always in favor of marriage, and the marriage must be considered valid until the contrary

Chelodi, *Jus Matrim.*, n. 113; Lehmkuhl, *Theol. Moral.*, II, n. 733; Ballerini-Palmieri, *Theol. Moral.*, VI, n. 619; D'Annibale, *Summula Moral.*, III, n. 444; Cerato, *Matrim.*, n. 80; Blat, *Comment.*, III, pars I, n. 483.

[15] Chelodi, *Jus Matrim.*, n. 113; Augustine, *A Commentary on Canon Law*, V, 236; Vermeerch-Creusen, *Epitome*, II, n. 371; Ayrinhac, *Marriage Legislation in the New Code*, n. 198; Fourneret, *Le Mariage Chrétien*, p. 123; Cance, *Droit Canonique*, p. 477; Bevilacqua, *Matrim.*, n. 388.

[16] Dr. O'Donnell in a very fine and scholarly article in the Irish Ecclesiastical Review (Oct. 1918) on this particular kind of error, points out that canons 1084, 1086 § 2 and 1092 have a direct bearing upon each other in as much as error about the essential properties of marriage does not render a marriage null, unless there has been a positive act of the will excluding one of the essential properties (c. 1086) or unless there has been a condition placed before marriage and this condition is contrary to the properties of marriage (c. 1092). In trying to prove that a marriage was null due to error about the essential properties of marriage, it must be determined whether there is to be applied canon 1086 § 2 or canon 1092.

had been proved in the external forum.[17] Moreover the act of excluding by a positive act of the will one of the essential properties of marriage is a positively bad act and hence this act must be proved.[18] But whether in each particular case there has been merely simple error of the intellect or whether there has been a positive act of the will, excluding one of the essential properties of marriage, or whether there has been a condition placed against one of these essential properties is a *res facti* and hence, involves the greatest difficulties for the court when it attempts to decide. It is indeed difficult enough to decide whether a *conditio sine qua non* against the essential properties of marriage has been placed. The question is even more difficult when it concerns the internal act of the will because then there must be considered the prevalence of the two intentions, one the general intention of contracting marriage according to the mind of Christ or according to the laws of nature, and the other the positive intention of excluding from the matrimonial consent, one of the essential properties of marriage.[19] Hence, the positive will of excluding one of the essential properties of marriage must not only be asserted but it must be conclusively proved.[20]

[17] Cappello, *De Sacram.*, III, n. 588; Blat., *Comment.*, III, pars I, n. 483; Cerato, *Matrim.*, n. 80; Farrugia, *De Matrim.*, n. 28; Chelodi, *Jus Matrim.*, n. 113; Gasparri, *De Matrim.*, n. 903; De Smet, *De Spons. et Matrim.*, n. 529.

[18] Blat, *Comment.*, III, pars I, n. 483.

[19] Wernz-Vidal, *Jus Canon.*, V, n. 492; Aryinhac, *Marriage Legislation in the New Code*, n. 202; Blat, *Comment.*, III, pars I, n. 483; Cappello, *De Sacram.*, III, n. 588; Chelodi, *Jus Matrim.*, n. 113.

[20] Ayrinhac, *Marriage Legislation in the New Code*, n. 202.

CHAPTER V

ERROR IN REGARD TO THE VALIDITY OF MARRIAGE

CANON 1085

Scientia aut opinio nullitatis matrimonii consensum matrimonialem necessario non excludit.

THIS canon lays down the principle that knowledge or opinion of the nullity of marriage does not necessarily exclude consent. Hence, in regard to the validity of marriage, the contracting party may err in a two fold manner.[1] First the contracting party may think that he or she is entering into a valid marriage, whereas there exists a diriment impediment which is unknown to the contracting party and this impediment renders the marriage objectively null.[2] Secondly, the contracting party may erroneously think that there exists an impediment, invalidating the marriage, whereas in reality, no diriment impediment exists at all.[3] Such an error in reference to the validity of the marriage, may be of law or of fact.[4]

For instance, in regard to error of law, in reference to the validity of the marriage, it is easy to imagine a case in which one of the parties believes that consanguinity in the fourth

[1] Wernz-Vidal, *Jus Canon.*, V, n. 493; Chelodi, *Jus Matrim.*, n. 114; Cappello, *De Sacram.*, III, n. 589; Cerato, *Matrim.*, n. 81; Vlaming, *Praelect.*, II, n. 530; Vermeerch-Creusen, *Epitome,* II, n. 372.

[2] Cappello, *De Sacram.*, III, n. 589; Farrugia, *De Matrim.*, n. 29; Blat, *Comment.*, III, pars I, n. 484; Augustine, *A Commentary on Canon Law,* V, 239; Petrovits, *The New Church Law on Marriage,* n. 409.

[3] Cerato, *Matrim,* n. 81; Cappello, *De Sacram.*, III, n. 589; Ayriniac, *Marriage Legislation in the New Code,* n. 199; Chelodi, *Jus Matrim.*, n. 114.

[4] Wernz-Vidal, *Jus Canon.*, V, n. 493; Noldin, *De Sacram.*, III, p. 639.

degree of the collateral line still invalidates marriage and hence, while in this error, contract marriage. On the other hand, a man may truly know that consanguinity in the third degree collateral line invalidates marriage, but err in regard to his relationship with his intended spouse. For he thus believes his marriage is null because he erroneously thinks his spouse is of the third degree of consanguinity where as in reality, she is not of the third degree but of the fourth. This last error is error of fact.[5]

Here in either case, the marriage will be valid or invalid, regardless of the knowledge or opinion of the contracting party, in reference to the validity of the marriage.[6] But in these two above cases, the question at issue will depend upon the existence or non-existence of a law at the time of the marriage, for if at the time of the marriage, there exists a law which renders one or both of the parties incapable of marrying, the law produces its juridic effects independently of the knowledge or opinion of the contracting parties.[7] Thus if a diriment impediment exists when the marriage has been entered into and this impediment has not been removed by proper dispensation, then even though one or both of the contracting parties err, the marriage is null and void.[8] On the contrary, should one or both of the parties erroneously think there exists an impediment invalidating their matrimonial union, the marriage is valid, regardless of their error. It may be well to state here, how-

[5] Blat, *Comment.*, III, pars III, I, n. 484; Vlaming, *Praelect.*, II, n. 530; Wernz-Vidal, *Jus Canon.*, V, n. 493; Cerato, *Matrim.*, n. 81.

[6] Cappello, *De Sacram.*, III, n. 589; Knecht, *Handbuck Des Katholischen Eherechts,* 562, Chelodi, *Jus Matrim.*, n. 116; Petrovits, *The New Church Law on Marriage,* n. 409; Augustine, *A Commentary on Canon Law,* V, 239.

[7] Wernz-Vidal, *Jus Canon.*, V, n. 493; De Becker, *De Spons. et Matrim.*, p. 60; Gougnard, *Tract. De Matrim.*, p. 160; Bevilacqua, *Matrim.*, n. 388; Cance, *Droit Canonique,* n. 312.

[8] Chelodi, *Jus Matrim.*, n. 114; Cappello, *De Sacram.*, III, n. 589; Vlaming, *Praelect.*, n. 530; Cerato, *Matrim.*, n. 81; Feije, *De Imped. et Disp. Matrim.*, n. 74; Blat, *Comment.*, III, pars I, n. 484.

ever, that where there exists an impediment which invalidates a marriage and the existence of this impediment is unknown to at least one of the contracting parties, so that one of these parties thus falsely believes that a true marriage exists, even though this marriage is invalid, it is considered in the eyes of the Church as a putative marriage.[9] Thus the legitimacy of the children is insured as long as these children have been born while one at least of the parents, rests in good faith in regard to the validity of his or her marriage.

As this canon points out, there is here rather a question of the influence of the knowledge or opinion concerning the validity of the marriage upon the consent of the contracting party or parties, rather than a question of error.[10] The point that this canon wishes to bring out is, that matrimonial consent is not necessarily excluded, even though one of the parties should err in regard to the existence of a diriment impediment at the time of the marriage. Hence, the marriage is invalid, due to the existence of the impediment, but it is not invalid on account of defect of matrimonial consent.[11] This is easily realized if one of the parties is in good faith. In this case where one of the parties is in good faith, matrimonial consent is given absolutely to the substance of the marriage and thus the diriment impediment renders the marriage invalid, but a real matrimonial consent has been given by the party in good faith.[12] That this is certainly recognized by the Church may

[9] Wernz-Vidal, *Jus Canon.*, V, n. 493; Chelodi, *Jus Matrim.*, n. 114; Vermeersch-Creusen, *Epitome*, II, n. 372; Vlaming, *Praelect.*, II, n. 530; Augustine, *A Commentary on Canon Law*, V, n. 239; Ayrinhac, *Marriage Legislation in the New Code*, n. 199; Blat, *Comment.*, III, pars I, n. 484.

[10] Cappello, *De Sacram.*, III, n. 589; Cance, *Droit Canonique*, n. 312; Fourneret, *Le Mariage Chrétien*, p. 124; Farrugia, *De Matrim.*, n. 29; Petrovits, *The New Church Law on Marriage*, n. 409.

[11] Gasparri, *De Matrim.*, II, n. 905; Gougnard, *Tract. De Matrim.*, p. 160; Benedictus XIV, *De Synodo Dioec.*, XIII, C. 22, n. 4; Chelodi, *Jus Matrim.*, n. 114.

[12] Wernz-Vidal, *Jus Canon.*, V, n. 650; Fourneret, *Le Mariage Chrétien*,

be ascertained from her policy of granting a "sanatio in radice." In such a case the Church does not demand the renewal of matrimonial consent. This clearly signifies that the Church considers that a true matrimonial consent had been given at the time of the marriage, but due to an existing impediment, the marriage thus lacked validity.[13]

It may easily happen that one of the contracting parties is in bad faith, that is, the party realizes the existence of the impediment and still attempts to contract marriage.[14] Even in this case, it can happen that such a party in bad faith, give truly and absolutely matrimonial consent, even though this consent is given in contempt of the law that prohibits such a marriage, for this diriment impediment does not directly affect the will but rather the person who is thus rendered incapable of marrying at the time of the marriage.[15]

But if, on the contrary, the contracting party under the influence of his or her error, thinks that marriage is entirely impossible and thus due to this error, wishes only to go through with a civil ceremony, or to enter into a mere fornicatious concubinage, then there is really lacking matrimonial consent.[16] But it must always be borne in mind, that there is here a question of fact and hence, whether the influence of error or opinion has been strong enough to destroy matrimonial consent, must be judged from a careful consideration of all the circumstances of the case. Nor is there given any presump-

p. 124; Cerato, *Matrim.*, n. 81; Augustine, *A Commentary on Canon Law*, V, 239.

[13] Cappello, *De Sacram.*, III, n. 589; Ayrinhac, *Marriage Legislation In The New Code*, n. 199; Wernz-Vidal, *Jus Canon.*, V, n. 493.

[14] Blat, *Comment.*, III, pars I, n. 484; Petrovits, *The New Church Law on Marriage*, n. 409; De Smet, *De Spons. et Matrim.*, n. 415.

[15] Chelodi, *Jus Canon.*, n. 114; Vermeersch-Creusen, *Epitome*, II, n. 372; Vlaming, *Praelect.*, II, n. 530; Gasparri, *De Matrim.*, II, n. 907.

[16] Cappello, *De Sacram.*, III, n. 589; Farrugia, *De Matrim.*, n. 29; De Becker, *De Spons. et Matrim.*, p. 60.

tion of law, in favor of one admitting this influence of error or opinion.[17]

What has been stated above in regard to an impediment to a marriage, made by ecclesiastical law, applies also to impediment of divine or natural law, since the consent of the will can also exist where these impediments of the divine and natural law render the marriage null. For these impediments, as in the case of ecclesiastical impediments, do not affect the will directly but only render the person incapable of marrying.[18] Thus canon 1085, makes no distinction in this matter and hence, this canon refers to all the impediments.

In practice, it may be said, that all those who marry with the knowledge of an existing diriment impediment, even though they have given a true matrimonial consent at the time of their marriage, should be induced to renew their consent, because, although it is possible for a true matrimonial consent to exist along with knowledge of an existing diriment impediment, however, in such a case, true consent may be wanting.[19]

It is controverted among canonists and theologians whether the *presumptio juris* militates against the existence of matrimonial consent in a civil marriage, Cappello thus distinguishes:

If it is a question of Catholics who have been well instructed in the fundamentals of their faith, it is to be presumed that such Catholics, when going before a civil magistrate, intend thus to go through with a mere civil ceremony and hence matrimonial consent is lacking.

If, on the other hand, there is a question of Catholics who have been brought up from youth without any religious training whatever, or who are indifferent entirely to their

[17] Wernz-Vidal, *Jus Canon.,* V, n. 493; Gougnard, *Tract. De Matrim.,* p. 161; Vermeersch-Creusen, *Epitome,* II, n. 372; Knecht, *Handbuck Des Katholischen Eherechts,* p. 563.

[18] Cappello, *De Sacram.,* III, n. 589; Cance, *Droit Canonique,* n. 312; Bevilacqua, *Matrim.,* n. 389; Vlaming, *Praelect.,* II, n. 530.

[19] Gougnard, *Tract. De Matrim.,* p. 161.

religion, or who have been badly instructed in their religion, the presumption is that they really intended a true marriage and hence, there exists a true matrimonial consent.

Finally, when considering non-Catholics who contract a civil marriage, the presumption is in favor of marriage and the existence of consent to this marriage. In more difficult cases, the matter should be referred to the Holy See. It is evident also, that in the foregoing distinctions there exists only a presumption of law which must necessarily give way to solid proof.[20]

[20] Cappello, *De Sacram.*, III, n. 590.

CHAPTER VI

CONVALIDATION OF MARRIAGE INVALID DUE TO ERROR

THERE are three ways in which marriage may be rendered null. First, when a diriment impediment exists at the time of the marriage and this impediment renders one or both of the contracting parties incapable of marrying; secondly, when consent is lacking on the part of one of the parties; thirdly when the prescribed form of the Catholic Church has not been adhered to. Just as there are three ways in which a marriage may be rendered null, so there are three kinds of simple convalidation of a marriage. It is clearly evident that the only kind of convalidation that is of concern here in reference to substantial error, is the convalidation of a marriage rendered null through lack of consent.[1]

In the case where there has been lack of consent, as happens where there is substantial error, the marriage is convalidated when the party who did not give consent, now gives his or her consent to the marriage.[2] However, it is necessary that the consent of the other party has not been withdrawn. Moreover, this consent of the other party once given is presumed to persevere unless its withdrawal is evident, that is, by a clear and positive revocation.[3] This lack of consent can only be supplied by the contracting party; no one else can supply this

[1] Cappello, *De Sacram.*, III, n. 844; D'Annibale, *Summula Moral.*, III, n. 504; Vlaming, *Praelect.*, II, n. 761.

[2] Gasparri, *De Matrim.*, II, n. 1383; Rosset, *De Matrim.*, n. 2973; Ballerini-Palmieri, *Theol. Moral.*, VI, n. 893; Chelodi, *Jus Matrim.*, n. 165.

[3] C. 1093.

consent, not even the Church by means of dispensation or in any other manner.[4]

In order to convalidate a marriage due to lack of consent, three things are necessary, that valid consent be given. First there must be the cessation of the cause that rendered the marriage null. Hence, in the case of error that has rendered a marriage null, it is necessary that the contracting party realize the error, because if this error is not realized, there still exists the cause that rendered the marriage null at the beginning and thus the marriage cannot be convalidated.[5]

The second thing necessary is a knowledge of the nullity of the marriage because without this knowledge, there cannot be a true and valid consent given to the matrimonial contract. Hence, without this new consent, all manifestations of marital love would be nothing else than a continuation and confirmation of the former invalid consent to the marriage.[6]

The third thing demanded is that the new consent be joined to the consent of the other party whose consent given at the beginning of the union, has thus perservered. Hence, in this way, there is brought about a mutual consent which is entirely essential for the existence of a true marriage.[7]

As soon as the person who has erred has realized the existence of the error that renders the marriage null, and gives consent to the matrimonial contract, the matrimonial union by its very nature, becomes healed, and a true and valid marriage exists. However, in regard to this convalidation, the Church,

[4] Cappello, *De Sacram.*, III, n. 846; Chelodi, *Jus Matrim.*, n. 165; Fourneret, *Le Mariage Chrétien*, p. 324; Wernz-Vidal, *Jus Canon.*, V, n. 648; Vlaming, *Praelect.*, II, n. 782.

[5] Cerato, *Matrim.*, n. 136; Feije, *De Imped. et Disp. Matrim.*, 760; Rosset, *De Matrim*, n. 2981; Augustine, *A. Commentary on Canon Law*, V, 387.

[6] Cappello, *De Sacram.*, III, n. 846; Chelodi, *Jus Matrim.*, n. 165; D'Annibale, *Summula Moral.*, III, n. 484; Ballerini-Palmieri, *Theol. Moral.*, VI, n. 894.

[7] Farrugia, *De Matrim.*, n. 343; Fourneret, *Le Mariage Chrétien*, p. 325; Wernz-Vidal *Jus Canon.*, V, n. 648; Bevilacqua, *Matrim.*, n. 561.

while she places no special condition, yet for the validity of such a union in some cases, demands that there be a renewal of consent on the part of both parties in the external forum.[8]

If the lack of consent, due to error was internal only, then the party who has not given consent to the marriage contract, has only to consent interiorily.[9]

This consent may be an expressed consent, or even a tacit consent suffices, namely; *per copulam cum affectu maritali sive per diuturniorem cohabitationem,* after the error has been detected by the erring party.[10] Hence, when the existence of error rendering marriage null has been occult, there is not required that consent be renewed publicly. Neither must the party who has not given a true consent to marriage, due to error, acquaint the other party of the existence of the error, nor of the nullity of their matrimonial union. Nor is it required that the party, who has erred, at the beginning of the matrimonial union, and now detects the error, procure the renewal of consent of the other party. The only thing necessary when the nullity of the marriage, due to error has been occult, is, that the party who has erred realize the error and consequently give consent privately to the marriage.[11]

But if the error rendering the marriage null, has been public, then it is necessary that there be a renewal of consent before a priest and two witnesses.[12] The reason for this is evident, since it rises from the very nature of marriage as a sacred contract and one of the sacraments instituted by Christ. Hence, when the error has been public, (that is when there are

[8] Cappello, *De Sacram.*, III, n. 847; Chelodi, *Jus Matrim.*, n. 165; Wernz-Vidal, *Jus Canon.*, V, n. 472.

[9] C. 1136, § 2.

[10] Schmalzgrueber, *Jus Eccles Univ.*, lib. IV, tit. I, n. 455.

[11] Wernz-Vidal, *Jus Canon.*, V, n. 472; Cappello, *De Sacram.*, III, n. 847; Fourneret, *Le Mariage Chrétien*, p. 325; Augustine, *A Commentary on Canon Law*, V, 387.

[12] C. 1136, § 3.

at least two witnesses, who are able to prove the existence of the marriage, due to error, in the external forum), no secret manifestation of consent or private convalidation suffices. For, just as the Church considers marriage a public and social act and hence, demands that it be celebrated publicly, so too, when there is question of convalidating a marriage that is null, due to public error, the Church demands that it be convalidated in the external forum, (that is by the prescribed forum of marriage).[13] Hence, as long as the marriage has been rendered null by public error, even though the parties have cohabited many years in ignorance of the error, even *per copulam libere et affectu maritali habitam,* and even though, once the error was detected, consent was given privately by the party who had erred, as long as consent was not publicly renewed, the marriage would be declared null and void by the ecclesiastical tribunal.[14]

If, as may happen, the error persists and is not recognized by the party who made the error at the time the marriage was contracted, the marriage still remains null. Even though the two parties are firmly convinced that they have contracted a true marriage, as long as this error continues, there can be no convalidation of the marriage. For in this case, a disposition to give consent would not suffice, namely, if the party who has not given consent, due to error, would immediately give consent, were he or she aware of the error that renders the marriage null. But there is demanded for validity, a true matrimonial consent *de praesenti.* Nor will marriage rendered null by substantial error become convalidated with the passing of time, since no marriage can be convalidated by time, which was nullified *de jure* at its very beginning. Hence, a true marriage can only exist by mutual consent and where

[13] Cappello, *De Sacram.,* III, n. 847.

[14] Benedictus XIV, *Quaest. Canon,* 317; Farrugia, *De Matrim.,* n. 343; Bevilacqua, *Matrim.,* n. 561; Blat, *Comment.,* III pars I, n. 697.

this mutual consent is lacking, prescription is of no avail in convalidating the marriage.[15]

As long as the party, then, who had made the error, does not give consent to the marriage, both parties, since there does not exist a true matrimonial bond between them, are free to contract other valid marriages. The reason for this is clear. Since the party who has erred did not give at the beginning a true matrimonial consent to the contract, there is no obligation of law to force the party to give a true consent now, since it is left to the erring party either to give consent or to have the marriage declared null by an ecclesiastic tribunal. Moreover, the other party, provided he or she did not fraudulently or deceitfully induce the erring party into the error, has a right also of either accepting the consent of the erring party or of demanding that the marriage be declared null.[16]

If, however, one of the parties has fraudulently or deceitfully induced the other party into error, then this guilty party is prohibited from withdrawing from the contract, if the injured party, now acquainted with the existence of the error, wishes to have the marriage convalidated, and there exists no other way to repair entirely the damage that has been done. Equity demands that in such a case the guilty party be denied the right to withdraw from the contract. For following the principles of strict justice, the guilty party cannot be held to a marriage that is absolutely invalid, due to the lack of consent on the part of the erring party. Moreover in strict justice, the guilty party cannot be held to a contract so defective, that it would deny him the right of withdrawing from it, while on the other hand, it would give the injured party the option of having the marriage convalidated or having the marriage de-

[15] Wernz-Vidal, *Jus Canon.*, V, n. 472; Cerato, *Matrim.*, n. 136; Chelodi, *Jus Matrim.*, n. 165; Vlaming, *Praelect.*, II, n. 531; Augustine, *A Commentary on Canon Law,* V, 387.

[16] Cappello, *De Sacram.*, III, n. 847; Wernz-Vidal, *Jus Canon.*, V, n. 472.

clared null. For marriage, by its very nature, being an indissoluble union, demands equal obligation on the part of both parties. However, in equity, the guilty party must be denied the right of withdrawal if the injured party wishes to convalidate the marriage, since in most cases, the injury which the guilty party has perpetrated by fraud, can only partially be atoned for by the dissolution of the marriage, while a true marriage in this case, seems to be the only means of repairing entirely the injury done. This is made more clear in considering a case where children have been born to such a union. The injured party who has been fraudulently led into error, once having realized the error, would naturally wish in most cases, that the marriage be convalidated for that seems the best thing for the welfare of the children. In this case, it would seem that this is the only means available to repair totally the damage done to the injured party. Hence the guilty party must be held to the contract.[17]

When, then, marriage is null, due to the existence of substantial error, once the existence of this error is ascertained by the erring party, both parties have the right to attack the marriage and demand a sentence of nullity from the ecclesiastical tribunal. However, the right to attack the marriage must be denied to one of the parties if this party was the cause of the error.[18] The burden of proof rests upon that party who thus attacks the validity of the marriage and if the nullity of the marriage cannot be established by sound juridicial proof, the sentence in the external forum must be given in favor of the validity of the marriage.[19]

Finally, it must be said, that the erring party loses all right

[17] Wernz-Vidal, *Jus Canon.*, V, n. 472; Rosset, *De Matrim.*, n. 1339; Schmalzgrueber, *Jus Eccles. Univ.*, lib. IV, tit. I, n. 422.

[18] C. 1971, § 1, n. 1; Jeije, *De Imped. et Disp. Matrim.*, n. 578; Gasparri, *De Matrim.*, II, n. 1479.

[19] Wernz-Vidal, *Jus Canon.*, V, n. 473.

to attack the validity of the marriage if, after the detection of the error, the party knowingly and freely rendered the *debitum conjugale*. And even though the consummation of the marriage were not able to be proved in the external forum, the right would also be lost to the erring party who willingly and freely continued to live the common life for some time after the error had been discovered. How long a time is required, for a free cohabitation after the detection of the error, to give a presumption that there has been a tacit ratification of the marriage is a thing not determined in law. It must be left to the prudent discretion of the ecclesiastical tribunal in each case. Some authors have maintained that only six months would suffice, while others demand a year and a half. However, no general law which might be followed, has been set down by the Church.[20]

[20] Wernz-Vidal, *Jus Canon.*, V, n. 473.

BIBLIOGRAPHY

Sources

Acta Apostolicae Sedis, Romae, 1909, ——.

Acta Sanctae Sedis, 41 vols., Romae, 1865-1908.

Bucceroni, Januarius, *Enchiridion Morale*, 4. ed., Romae, 1905.

Codicis Iuris Canonici Fontes, cura Emi. Petri Card. Gasparri editi, 5 vols., Romae, 1926-1930.

Collectanea S. Congregationis de Propaganda Fide, 2 vols., Romae, 1907.

Concilii Plenarii Baltimorensis III (1884), Baltimore, 1886.

Corpus Juris Canonici, ed. Richter-Friedberg, 2 vols., Lipsiae, 1922.

Corpus Iuris Civilis: Institutiones, recognovit P. Krueger; *Digesta, recognovit* Th. Mommsen, retractavit P. Krueger, vol. I, Berolini, 1928; *Codex Justinianus*, recognovit et retractavit P. Krueger, vol. II, Berolini, 1929; *Novellae*, recognovit R. Schoell, opus Schoelli morte interceptum absolvit G. Kroll, vol. III, Berolini, 1928.

Hardouin, J., *Conciliorum Collectio Regia Maxima*, 12 vols., Parisiis, 1715.

Mansi, Joannes, *Sacrorum Conciliorum Nova et Amplissima Collectio*, 53 vols., Paris-Arnhem-Leipsig, 1901-1927.

Thesaurus Resolutionum Sacrae Congregationis Concilii, 167 vols., Romae, 1718-1908.

Authors

A Dictionary of Christian Antiquity, 2 vols., London, 1890.

Allard, P., *Les Esclaves Chrétiens*, 3. ed., Paris, 1900.

Allard, P., *Les Origen Du Servage En France*, Paris, 1913.

Alphonsus de Legorio, St., *Theologia Moralis*, 2 vols., Turin, 1888.

Ayrinhac, H. A., *General Legislation in the New Code of Canon Law*, New York, 1923.

Ayrinhac, H. A., *Marriage Legislation in the New Code of Canon Law*, New York, 1918.

[Bachofen], Charles Augustine, *A Commentary on the New Code of Canon Law*, 4 ed., 8 vols., St. Louis, 1918-1929.

Ballerini, Antonius, *S. Ambrosii Opera Omnia*, 6 vols., Milan, 1875.

Ballerini, A.-Palmieri, D., *Opus Theologicum Morale*, 3. ed., 7 vols., Prati, 1898-1901.

Benedictus XIV, *De Synodo Dioecesana*, 2 vols., Romae, 1806.

Bangen, A., *Instructio Practica De Sponsalibus Et Matrimonino*, Rome, 1858.

Bernardini a Piconio, *Opera Omnia*, Tomus IV, Parisiis, 1872.

Bernardus Papiensis, *Summa Decretalium*, ed. Th. Laspeyres, Ratisbonae, 1860.

Bevilacqua, A., *Trattato Dommatico, Guiridico E Morale Sul Matrimonino Cristiano*, 2. ed., Rome, 1918.

Billot, Ludovicus, *De Ecclesiae Sacramentis Commentarius in Tertiam Partem S. Thomae,* 2. ed., 2 vols., Romae, 1897.

Billuart, Carolus, *Cursus Theologiae iuxta Mentem Divi Thomae,* 20 vols., Parisiis, 1827-1831.

Bingham, J., *Origenes Ecclesiastical or Antiquities of the Christian Church,* 9 vols., Lind, 1845.

Blat, Albertus, *Commentarium Textus Codicis Iuris Canonici,* 6 vols., vol. III, *De Sacramentis, Romae,* 1921-1927.

Bonfante, P., *Istituzioni Di Diritto Romano,* 7. ed., Romae, 1921.

Buckland, W. W., *A Text-book of Roman Law,* Cambridge, 1921.

Cance, A., *Le Code De Droit Canonique,* 10 vols., 6. ed., Paris, 1930.

Cappello, Felix M., *Tractatus Canonico-Moralis De Sacramentis,* vol. III, *De Matrimonio,* 2. ed., Romae, 1927.

Carrière, S., *Praelectiones theological majores de Matrimonio,* Paris, 1837.

Catholic Encyclopedia, 15 vols., New York, 1907-1912.

Cerato, Prosdocimus, *Matrimonium a Codice I. C. Integre Desumptum,* 4. ed., Patavii, 1927.

Chelodi, Joannes, *Jus Matrimoniale iuxta Codicem Iuris Canonici,* 3. ed., Tridenti, 1921.

Cogliolo, Pietro, *Manuale delle Fonti del Diritto Romano,* 2. ed., Torino, 1911.

D'Annibale, Josephus, *Summula Theologiae Moralis,* 3. ed., 3 vols., 1892.

De Angelis, Philippus, *Praelectiones Iuris Canonici, ad Methodum Decretalium Gregorii IX Exactae,* 6 vols., Romae, 1880.

De Becker, Julius, *De Sponsalibus et Matrimonio Praelectiones Canonicae,* Bruxellis, 1896.

De Smet, Aloysius, *Tractatus Theologico-Canonicus de Sponsalibus et Matrimonio,* 4. ed., Brugis, 1927.

Döllinger, J., *Hippolytus and Callistus,* Edinburgh, 1876.

Esmein, A., *Le Mariage en Droit Canonique,* 2 vols., Paris, 1891.

Farrugia, P. Nicolaus, *De Matrimonio et Causis Matrimonialibus, tractatus canonico-moralis iuxta Codicem Iuris Canonici,* Romae, 1924.

Feije, Henricus, *De impedimentis et Dispensationibus Matrimonialibus,* 3. ed., Lovanii, 1885.

Ferrini, C., *Manuale Di Pandette,* 3. ed., Milan, 1917.

Fourneret, P., *Le Mariage Chrétien,* 4. ed., Paris, 1925.

Freisen, J., *Geschichte des Canonischen Eherechts,* Paderborn, 1893.

Fulton, J., *The Laws of Marriage,* London, 1883.

Funk, Francis Xavier, *A Manual of Church History,* translated from the German by P. Perciballi, edited by W. H. Kent, 2 vols., London, 1914.

Gasparri, Petrus, *Tractatus Canonicus de Matrimonio,* 3. ed., 2 vols., Parisiis, 1904.

Genicot, Soloman, *Theologiae Morales Institutiones,* ed., 10 Brussels, 1922.

Girard, P., *Manuel Elémentaire De Droit Romain,* 7. ed., Paris, 1924.

Gothofredus, Dionysius, *Corpus Iuris Civilis Romani, in quo Institutiones, Digesta ad Codicem Florentinum Emendata, Codex Item et Novellae, cum Notis Integris,* 9. ed., 2 vols., Coloniae Munatianae, 1781.

Gougnard, A., *Tractatus De Matrimonio,* 7. ed., Mecklin, 1931.

Hefele, K., *Conciliengeschichte,* 2. ed., 9 vols., Freiburg, 1873-1890.

Hostiensis (Henricus de Segusio), *Commentaria in V Libros Decretalium,* 3 vols., Venetiis, 1581.

Howard, George Elliot, *The History of Matrimonial Institutions,* 3 vols., Chicago, 1904.

Hurter, H., *Theologiae Dogmaticae,* 6. ed., 3 vols., Oeniponte, 1889.

Kenrick, Francis P., *Theologia Moralis,* 2 vols., Mechliniae, 1861.

Knecht, A., *Handbuch Des Katholeschen Eherechts,* 1. ed., Freiburg, im Breisgan, 1928.

Könings, Antonius, *Theologia Moralis,* 7. ed., 2 vols., Neo-Eboraci, 1889.

Lacroix, J., *Theologiae Morales,* Paris, 1674.

Lancelotti, Giovanni, *Institutiones Iuris Canonici,* Lugduni, 1579.

Leage, R. W., *Roman Private Law,* London, 1924.

Lehmkuhl, Augustinus, *Theologia Moralis,* 3. ed., 2 vols., Friburgi Brisgoviae, 1886.

Linneborn, J., *Grundris des Eherechts,* Paderborn, 1922.

Lombard, Peter, *Libri IV Sententiarum,* 2 vols., Florence, 1916.

Mansella, Joseph, *De Impedimentis Matrimonium Dirimentibus ac de Processu Iudiciali in Causis Matrimonialibus,* Romae, 1881.

McHugh, John-Callan, Charles, *Catechism of the Council of Trent for Parish Priests,* New York, 1923.

Michel, *Questions Pratiques sur le Mariage dans les Missions,* Maison-Carree, 1903.

Migne, Jacques Paul, *Patrologiae Cursus Completus, Series Graeca,* 161 vols., Parisiis, 1858-1864.

Migne, Jacques Paul, *Patrologiae Cursus Completus, Series Latina,* 221 vols., Parisiis, 1844-1855.

Noldin, H., *De Principiis Theologiae Moralis, Scholarum Usui accommodavit, recognovit et emendavit A. Schmitt,* 20. ed., 3 vols., Oeniponte, 1929.

Noldin, H., *De Iure Matrimoniali iuxta Codicem Iuris Canonici, Scholarum Usui Accommodavit,* Lincii, 1919.

Ojetti, Benedictus, *Synopsis Rerum Moralium et Juris Pontificii,* 3. ed., 4 vols., Romae, 1911.

Palmieri, Dominicus, *Tractatus de Matrimonio Christiano,* Romae, 1880.

Perrone, Joannes, *De Matrimonio Christiano,* 3 vols., Leodii, 1861.

Perrone, Joannes, *Praelectiones Theologicae,* Tomus VIII, 2. ed., Romae, 1844.

Pesch, Christianus, *Tractatus Dogmatici,* 9 vols., Friburgi Brisgoviae, 1897.

Petrovits, Joseph J. C., *The New Church Law on Matrimony,* 2. ed., Philadelphia, 1926.

Petrus Lombardus, *Petri Lombardi Libri IV Sententiarum* studio et cura PP. Collegii S. Bonaventurae in lucem editi, 2. ed., 2 vols., Ad Claras Aquas, 1916.

Pichler, Vitus, *Epitome Iuris Canonici*, 2 vols., Venetiis, 1755.

Pirhing, Ernicus, *Jus Canonicum Nova Methodo Explicatum*, 2 vols., Dilingae, 1678.

Prümmer, Dominicus, *Manuale Theologiae Moralis*, 3. ed., 3 vols., Friburgi Brisgoviae, 1923.

Raymundus de Peneforte, *Summa*, Veronae, 1744.

Reiffenstuel, Anacletus, *Jus Canonicum Universum*, 4 vols., Romae, 1838.

Rosset, M., *De Sacramento Matrimonii*, 6 vols., Parisiis, 1895-1896.

Sanchez, Thomas, *De Sancto Matrimonii Sacramento Disputationum, Tomi Tres*, Lugduni, 1669.

Santi, Franciscus, *Praelectiones Iuris Canonici*, 5 vols., Ratisbonae, 1884.

Scavini, Petrus, *Theologia Moralis Universa ad Mentem S. Alphonsi M. de Ligorio*, 9. ed., 4 vols., Mediolani, 1869.

Schmalzgrueber, Franciscus, *Jus Ecclesiasticum Universum*, 12 vols., Romae, 1844.

Schulte, J. F., von, *Die Geschichte der Quellen und Literatur des Canonischen Rechts von Gratian bis Papst Gregor IX*, 3 vols., Stuttgart, 1875-1880.

Schulte, von, F. J., *Lehrbuch des Katholischen Kirchenrechts*, Giessen, 1873.

Schulte, J. F., von, *Die Glosse zum Dekret Gratian's von ihren Anflangen bis auf die jüngsten Ausgaben*, 4. ed., Vienna, 1872.

Sherman, C. P., *Roman Law in the Modern World*, 3 vols., New York, 1924.

Sohm, Rudolph-Ledlie, J. C., *The Institutes, A Text-book of the History and System of Roman Private Law*, London, 1907.

Soto, Dominicus, *In Quartum* (quem vocant) *Sententiarum*, Tomi I, II, Venetiis, 1575.

Tancredus, *Tancredi Summa de Matrimonio*, edited by A. Wunderlich, Gottingae, 1841.

Tanquery, A., *Synopsis Theologiae Moralis Et Pastoralis*, 3 vols., Paris, 1925.

Thomas Aquinas, *Summa Theologica*, 2. Roman edition, Romae, 1894.

Thomas Aquinas, *Commentaria in Omnes D. Pauli Apostoli Epistolas*, nova editio, Tomus I, Parisiis, 1870.

Tirini, Jacobus, *Commentarius in Universam S. Scripturam*, 5 vols., Trurini, 1882-1884.

Tribes, T., *Handbuch Des Kanonischen Eherechts*, Bresla, 1927.

Vecchiotti, S. M., *Tractatus Canonicus de Matrimonio*, Taurini, 1868.

Veermeersch, Arthurus, *Commentaria de Formulis Facultatum S. C. de Prop. Fide*, Brugis, 1922.

Vermeersch, Arthurus, *De Casu Apostoli seu De Fidei Privilegio*, Brugis, 1911.

Vermeersch, A.-Creusen, J., *Epitome Iuris Canonici*, 3. ed., 3 vols., Mechliniae-Romae, 1927.

Vlaming, Th. M., *Praelectiones Iuris Matrimonii,* 3. ed., 2 vols., Bussum in Hollandia, 1921.

Wallon, J., *Histoire De L'Esclavage Dans L'Antiquite,* Paris, 1900.

Waterworth, J., *The Canons and Decrees of the Sacred and Oecumenical Council of Trent, with Essays on the External and Internal History of the Council,* London, 1848.

Wernz, Franciscus X., *Jus Decretalium,* 2. ed., 6 vols., Prati, 1912.

Wernz, F. X.-Vidal, Petrus, *Jus Canonicum ad Codicis Normam Exactum,* 3 vols., vol. V, *Jus Matrimoniale,* Romae, 1923-1928.

Westermarck, Edward, *The History of Human Marriage,* 5. ed., 3 vols., 1922.

Winslow, Francis Joseph, *Vicars and Prefects Apostolic,* Washington, 1924.

Wirceburgensis, *Theologia Dogmatica,* Tomus X, *De Sacramento Matrimonii,* 3. ed., 10 vols., Parisiis, 1880.

Woywod, S., *A Practical Commentary on the Code of Canon Law,* 2. ed., 2 vols., New York, 1926.

Zitelli, Zephyrinus, *De Dispensationibus Matrimonialibus recentissimas sac.* urbis congreg. resolutiones Commentarii, Romae, 1887.

UNIVERSITAS CATHOLICA AMERICAE

WASHINGTONII, D. C.

FACULTAS JURIS CANONICI

1932

No. 82

DEUS LUX MEA

TITULI

QUOS

AD DOCTORATUS GRADUM

IN

JURE CANONICO

APUD UNIVERSITATEM CATHOLICAM AMERICAE

CONSEQUENDUM

PUBLICE PROPUGNABIT

HERIBERTUS T. RIMLINGER

SACERDOS DIOECESIS WILMINGTONIENSIS

JURIS CANONICI LICENTIATUS

HORA IX, A. M. DIE XXIII MAII MCMXXXII

TITULI

IN IURE CANONICO

I.	De Dissertatione.	
II.	De Juris Canonici Historia.	
III.	Canones 1-7	De Canonibus Introductoriis.
IV.	Canones 8-24	De Legibus Ecclesiasticis.
V.	Canones 25-30	De Consuetudine.
VI.	Canones 31-35	De Temporis Supputatione.
VII.	Canones 36-62	De Rescriptis.
VIII.	Canones 118-123	De Iuribus et Privilegiis Clericorum
IX.	Canones 492-498	De Erectione et Suppressione Religionis, Provinciae, Domus.
X.	Canones 499-517	De Superioribus et de Capitulis.
XI.	Canones 518-530	De Confessariis et de Cappellanis.
XII.	Canones 531-537	De Bonis Temporalibus Eorumque Administratione.
XIII.	Canones 539-541	De Postulatu.
XIV.	Canones 542-552	De Requisitis ut Quis in Novitiatum Admittatur.
XV.	Canones 553-571	De Novitiorum Institutione.
XVI.	Canones 572-586	De Professione Religiosa.
XVII.	Canones 587-591	De Ratione Studiorum in Religionibus Clericalibus.
XVIII.	Canones 592-612	De Obligationibus Religiosorum.
XIX.	Canones 613-625	De Privilegiis Religiosorum.
XX.	Canones 757-779	De Baptismo.
XXI.	Canones 1012-1018	De Matrimonio in Genere.
XXII.	Canones 1050-1066	De Impedimentibus Impedientibus.
XXIII.	Canones 1067-1080	De Impedimentis Dirimentibus.
XXIV.	Canones 1094-1103	De Forma Celebrationis Matrimonii.
XXV.	Canones 1104-1107	De Matrimonio Conscientiae.
XXVI.	Canones 1406-1408	De Fidei Professione.
XXVII.	Canones 1552-1568	De Notione Iudicii et de Foro Competenti.
XXVIII.	Canones 1572-1593	De Tribunali Ordinario Primae Instantiae.
XXIX.	Canones 1608-1645	De Disciplina in Tribunalibus Servanda.
XXX.	Canones 1646-1666	De Partibus in Causa.
XXXI.	Canones 1706-1725	De Causae Introductione.
XXXII.	Canones 1726-1731	De Litis Instantia.
XXXIII.	Canones 1750-1753	De Confessione Partium.
XXXIV.	Canones 1770-1781	De Examine Testium.
XXXV.	Canones 1812-1824	De Probatione per Instrumenta.
XXXVI.	Canones 2162-2167	De Translatione Parochorum.
XXXVII.	Canones 2195-2198	De Natura Delicti.

XXXVIII.	Canones 2214-2220	De Poenis in Genere.
XXXIX.	Canones 2241-2285	De Censuris.
XL.	Canones 2306-2311	De Poenalibus Remediis.

XLI. The Periods of Roman Law.
XLII. The Sources of Roman Law.
XLIII. Personality.
XLIV. Slavery.
XLV. Citizenship.
XLVI. Patria Potestas.
XLVII. Personae in Manu.
XLVIII. Tutela et Cura.
XLIX. Personae in Mancipio.
L. Ownership.
LI. De Obligationibus in Genere.
LII. De Obligationibus Extra-Contractualibus.
LIII. Furtum.
LIV. Damnum Iniuria Datum.
LV. De Actionibus.

AMERICAN CHURCH—CIVIL LAW

LVI. Juridical Status of the Church in the United States.
LVII. Methods of Holding Church Property.
LVIII. Tax Exemption.
LIX. Marriage.
LX. Cemeteries.

Vidit Facultas:

VALENTINUS T. SCHAAF, O.F.M., J.C.D., Vice-Decanus.
LUDOVICUS H. MOTRY, S.T.D., J.C.D., a Secretis.
FRANCISCUS J. LARDONE, S.T.D., J.U.D.
JOHN McDILL FOX, A.B., LL.B.

Vidit Rector Magnificus Universitatis:

JACOBUS HUGO RYAN, S.T.D., PH.D., LL.D., LITT.D.

BIOGRAPHICAL NOTE

HERBERT T. RIMLINGER was born September 28, 1905, at Wilmington, Delaware. He attended St. Elizabeth's Parochial School, Wilmington, and St. Charles College, Catonsville, Maryland. His philosophical and theological studies were made at St. Mary's Seminary, Baltimore, Maryland, from which institution he received the degree of Bachelor of Arts. In the fall of 1930 he entered the Catholic University to pursue a graduate course of studies in Canon Law. He was ordained to the Holy Priesthood on June 12, 1930.

CANON LAW STUDIES

1. Freriks, Rev. Celestine A., C.PP.S., J.C.D., Religious Congregations in Their External Relations, 121 pp., 1916.
2. Galliher, Rev. Daniel M., O.P., J.C.D., Canonical Elections, 117 pp., 1917.
3. Borkowski, Rev. Aurelius L., O.F.M., De Confraternitatibus Ecclesiasticis, 136 pp., 1918.
4. Castillo, Rev. Cayo, J.C.D., Disertacion Historico-canonica sobre la Potestad del Cabildo en Sede Vacante o Impedida del Vicario Capitular, 99 pp., 1919 (1918).
5. Kubelbeck, Rev. William J., S.T.B., J.C.D., The Sacred Penitentiaria and Its Relations to Faculties of Ordinaries and Priests, 129 pp., 1918.
6. Petrovits, Rev. Joseph J. C., S.T.D., J.C.D., The New Church Law on Matrimony, X-461 pp., 1919.
7. Hickey, Rev. John J., S.T.B., J.C.D., Irregularities and Simple Impediments in the New Code of Canon Law, 100 pp., 1920.
8. Klekotka, Rev. Peter J., S.T.B., J.C.D., Diocesan Consultors, 179 pp., 1920.
9. Wannenmacher, Rev. Francis, J.C.D., The Evidence in Ecclesiastical Procedure Affecting the Marriage Bond, 1920. (Not Printed.)
10. Golden, Rev. Henry Francis, J.C.D., Parochial Benefices in the New Code, IV-119 pp., 1921. (Printed 1925.)
11. Koudelka, Rev. Charles J., J.C.D., Pastors, Their Rights and Duties According to the New Code of Canon Law, 211 pp., 1921.
12. Melo, Rev. Antonius, O.F.M., J.C.D., De Exemptione Regularium, X-188 pp., 1921.
13. Schaaf, Rev. Valentine Theodore, O.F.M., S.T.B., J.C.D., The Cloister, X-180 pp., 1921.
14. Burke, Rev. Thomas Joseph, S.T.B., J.C.D., Competence in Ecclesiastical Tribunals, IV-117 pp., 1922.
15. Leech, Rev. George Leo, J.C.D., A Comparative Study of the Constitution "Apostolicae Sedis" and the "Codex Juris Canonici," 179 pp., 1922.
16. Motry, Rev. Hubert Louis, S.T.D., J.C.D., Diocesan Faculties according to the Code of Canon Law, II-167 pp., 1922.
17. Murphy, Rev. George Lawrence, J.C.D., Delinquencies and Penalties in the Administration and the Reception of the Sacraments, IV-121 pp., 1923.
18. O'Reilly, Rev. John Anthony, S.T.B., J.C.D., Ecclesiastical Sepulture in the New Code of Canon Law, II-129 pp., 1923.
19. Michalicka, Rev. Wenceslas Cyrill, O.S.B., J.C.D., Judicial Procedure in Dismissal of Clerical Exempt Religious, 107 pp., 1923.
20. Dargin, Rev. Edward Vincent, S.T.B., J.C.D., Reserved Cases According to the Code of Canon Law, IV-103 pp., 1924.
21. Godfrey, Rev. John A., S.T.B., J.C.D., The Right of Patronage According to the Code of Canon Law, 153 pp., 1924.
22. Hagedorn, Rev. Francis Edward, J.C.D., General Legislation on Indulgences, II-154 pp., 1924.

23. King, Rev. James Ignatius, J.C.D., The Administration of the Sacraments to Dying Non-Catholics, V-141 pp., 1924.
24. Winslow, Rev. Francis Joseph, A.F.M., J.C.D., Vicars and Prefects Apostolic, IV-149 pp., 1924.
25. Correa, Rev. Jose Servelion, S.T.L., J.C.D., La Potestad Legislativa de la Iglesia Católica, IV-127 pp., 1925.
26. Dugan, Rev. Henry Francis, M.A., J.C.D., The Judiciary Department of the Diocesan Curia, 87 pp., 1925.
27. Keller, Rev. Charles Frederick, S.T.B., J.C.D., Mass Stipends, 167 pp., 1925.
28. Paschang, Rev. John Linus, J.C.D., The Sacramentals According to the Code of Canon Law, 129 pp., 1925.
29. Piontek, Rev. Cyrillus, O.F.M., S.T.B., J.C.D., De Indulto Exclaustrationis necnon Saecularizationis, XIII-289 pp., 1925.
30. Kearney, Rev. Richard Joseph, S.T.B., J.C.D., Sponsors at Baptism According to the Code of Canon Law, IV-127 pp., 1925.
31. Bartlett, Rev. Chester Joseph, A.M., LL.B., J.C.D., The Tenure of Parochial Property in the United States of America, V-108 pp., 1926.
32. Kilker, Rev. Adrian Jerome, J.C.D., Extreme Unction, V-425 pp., 1926.
33. McCormick, Rev. Robert Emmett, J.C.D., Confessors of Religious, VIII-266 pp., 1926.
34. Miller, Rev. Newton Thomas, J.C.D., Founded Masses According to the Code of Canon Law, VII-93 pp., 1926.
35. Roelker, Rev. Edward G., S.T.D., J.C.D., Principles of Privilege According to the Code of Canon Law, XI-166 pp., 1926.
36. Bakalarczyk, Rev. Richardus, M.I.C., J.U.D., De Novitiatu, VIII-208 pp., 1927.
37. Pizzuti, Rev. Lawrence, O.F.M., J.U.L., De Parochis Religiosis, 1927. (Not Printed.)
38. Bliley, Rev. Nicholas Martin, O.S.B., J.C.D., Altars According to the Code of Canon Law, XIX-132 pp., 1927.
39. Brown, Brendan Francis, A.B., LL.M., J.U.D., The Canonical Juristic Personality with Special Reference to its Status in the United States of America, V-212 pp., 1927.
40. Cavanaugh, Rev. William Thomas. C.P., J.U.D., The Reservation of the Blessed Sacrament, VIII-101 pp., 1927.
41. Doheny, Rev. William J., C.S.C., A.B., J.U.D., Church Property: Modes of Acquisition, X-118 pp., 1927.
42. Feldhaus, Rev. Aloysius H., C.PP.S., J.C.D., Oratories, IX-141 pp., 1927.
43. Kelly, Rev. James Patrick, A.B., J.C.D., The Jurisdiction of the Simple Confessor, X-208 pp., 1927.
44. Neuberger, Rev. Nicholas J., J.C.D., Canon 6 or the Relation of the Codex Juris Canonici to the Preceding Legislation, V-95 pp., 1927.
45. O'Keeffe, Rev. Gerald Michael, J.C.D., Matrimonial Dispensations, Powers of Bishops, Priests, and Confessors, VIII-232 pp., 1927.
46. Quigley, Rev. Joseph, A.M., A.B., J.C.D., Condemned Societies, 139 pp., 1927.
47. Zaplotnik, Rev. Ioannes Leo, J.C.D., De Vicariis Foraneis, X-142 pp., 1927.

48. Duskie, Rev. John Aloysius, A.B., J.C.D., The Canonical Status of the Orientals in the United States, VIII-196 pp., 1928.
49. Hyland, Rev. Francis Edward, J.C.D., Excommunication, Its Nature, Historical Development and Effects, VIII-181 pp., 1928.
50. Reinmann, Rev. Gerald Joseph, O.M.C., J.C.D., The Third Order Secular of Saint Francis, 201 pp., 1928.
51. Schenk, Rev. Francis J., J.C.D., The Matrimonial Impediments of Mixed Religion and Disparity of Cult, XVI-318 pp., 1929.
52. Coady, Rev. John Joseph, S.T.D., J.U.D., A.M., The Appointment of Pastors, VIII-150 pp., 1929.
53. Kay, Rev. Thomas Henry, J.C.D., Competence in Matrimonial Procedure, VIII-164 pp., 1929.
54. Turner, Rev. Sidney Joseph, C.P., J.U.D., The Vow of Poverty, XLIX-217 pp., 1929.
55. Kearney, Rev. Raymond A., A.B., S.T.D., J.C.D., The Principles of Delegation, VII-149 pp., 1929.
56. Conran, Rev. Edward James, A.B., J.C.D., The Interdict, V-163 pp., 1930.
57. O'Neil, Rev. William H., J.C.D., Papal Rescripts of Favor, VII-218 pp.,
58. Bastnagel, Rev. Clement Vincent, J.U.D., The Appointment of Parochial Adjutants and Assistants, XV-257 pp., 1930.
59. Ferry, Rev. William A., A.B., J.C.D., Stole Fees, X-107 pp., 1930.
60. Costello, Rev. John Michael, A.B., J.C.D., Domicile and Quasi-Domicile, VII-201 pp., 1930.
61. Kremer, Rev. Michael Nicholas, A.B., S.T.B., J.C.D., Church Support in the United States, VI-136 pp., 1930.
62. Angulo, Rev. Luis, C.M., J.C.D., Legislación de la Iglesia sobre la intención en la aplicación de la Santa Misa, VII-104 pp., 1931.
63. Frey, Rev. Wolfgang Norbert, O.S.B., A.B., J.C.D., The Act of Religious Profession, VIII-174 pp., 1931.
64. Roberts, Rev. James Brendan, A.B., J.C.D., The Banns of Marriage, XIV-140 pp., 1931.
65. Ryder, Rev. Raymond Aloysius, A.B., J.C.D., Simony, IX-151 pp., 1931.
66. Campagna, Rev. Angelo, Ph.D., J.U.D., Il Vicario Generale del Vescovo, VII-205 pp., 1931.
67. Cox, Rev. Joseph Godfrey, A.B., J.C.D., The Administration of Seminaries, VI-124 pp., 1931.
68. Gregory, Rev. Donald J., J.U.D., The Pauline Privilege, XV-165 pp., 1931.
60. Donohue, Rev. John F., J.C.D., The Impediment of Crime, VIII-110 pp., 1931.
70. Dooley, Rev. Eugene A., O.M.I., J.C.D., Church Law on Sacred Relics, IX-143 pp., 1931.
71. Orth, Rev. Clement Raymond, O.M.C., J.C.D., The Approbation of Religious Institutes, 171 pp., 1931.
72. Pernicone, Rev. Joseph M., A.B., J.C.D., The Ecclesiastical Prohibition of Books, XII-267 pp., 1932.
73. Clinton, Rev. Connell, A.B., J.C.L., The Paschal Precept, 1932.
74. Donnelly, Rev. Francis B., A.M., S.T.L., J.C.L., The Diocesan Synod, 1932

75. TORRENTE, REV. CAMILO, C.M.F., J.C.L., Las Processiones Sagradas, 1932.
76. MURPHY, REV. EDWIN J., C.PP.S., J.C.L., Suspension Ex Informata Conscientia, 1932.
77. MACKENZIE, REV. ERIC F., A.M., S.T.L., J.C.L., The Delict of Heresy in its Commission, Penalization, Absolution, 1932.
78. LYONS, REV. AVITUS E., S.T.B., J.C.L., The Collegiate Tribunal of First Instance, 1932.
79. CONNOLLY, REV. THOMAS A., J.C.L., Appeals, 1932.
80. SANGMEISTER, REV. JOSEPH V., A.B., J.C.L., Force and Fear as Precluding Matrimonial Consent, 1932.
81. JAEGER, REV. LEO A., A.B., J.C.L., The Administration of Vacant and Quasi-Vacant Episcopal Sees in the United States, 1932.
82. RIMLINGER, REV. HERBERT T., J.C.L., Error Invalidating Matrimonial Consent, 1932.
83. BARRETT, REV. JOHN D. M., S.S., J.C.L., Comparative Study of the Third Plenary Council and the Code, 1932.

www.ingramcontent.com/pod-product-compliance
Lightning Source LLC
LaVergne TN
LVHW050157080826
844660LV00012B/307

* 9 7 8 0 8 1 3 2 2 2 7 1 4 *